STUDY
of the
HOLY
SPIRIT

STUDY
of the
HOLY
SPIRIT

by

William Edward Biederwolf

Foreword by

William G. Moorehead

KREGEL PUBLICATIONS
Grand Rapids, Michigan 49501

Study of the Holy Spirit by William Edward Biederwolf. Published by Kregel Publications, a division of
Kregel, Inc. All rights reserved.

Library of Congress Cataloging in Publication Data

Biederwolf, William E. (William Edward),
   1867-1939. Study of the Holy Spirit.

   Originally published: A Help to the Study of the
Holy Spirit. 4th ed. Boston: J.H. Earle, c1903.
   Bibliography: p.
   1. Holy Spirit. I. Title.
BT121.B5 1985   231'.3   84-25099
ISBN 0-8254-2244-2

CONTENTS

6   **Contents**

FOREWORD

OUR age is distinguished for its earnestness of study in the doctrine of the Holy Spirit. The last quarter of a century has been remarkable for the productiveness of books on this great subject. Naturally, there is considerable diversity as to the relative value of works on the person and the functions of the spirit. Some confine themselves to a single phase of the Spirit's activity, while others treat of Him both as to His person and work. In all, however, there is apparent the desire to be true to the Scripture, which must always remain the one unchanging source of knowledge on this as on all other parts of revealed truth. There is manifest likewise the honest effort to be helpful to Christians who long to know more of the gracious Spirit without whose presence and assistance they feel themselves powerless as witnesses for Christ.

However copiously treated, the great theme is not exhausted, nor can it be. For it is with one of the Persons of the Godhead we are dealing, hence the theme is an infinite one. Accordingly, fresh studies on it are always in place. No one book nor all books combined have here spoken the last word. This mine of truth will be as productive for the generations to come as it has been in the ages past. Since the Spirit is the Author of that mighty change in men commonly called regeneration, since He is the fountain of all true holiness of life in the saved, since it is He who baptizes believers into the one Body, and is

Himself the gracious Habitant of the body, fitting it
by His presence and His grace for its glorious destiny,
every new effort to shed light on His blessed work
should be welcomed with gladness by the people of
God.

It is with sincere pleasure that this book by the
Rev. W. E. Biederwolf is commended to Christian
people. Certain features in it are noteworthy. First,
it is conservative. By this is not meant that it deals
only with those phases of the Spirit's work that are
universally recognized and accepted, while those more
recondite and difficult are passed over in silence, for
the author grapples with some of the most mysterious
and abstruse features of the great problem. What
is meant is, that the author is ruled by a wise caution
in his treatment of the theme, and particularly in his
expositions. He brings his views and the views of
others also to the word of God as the arbiter and
final test. There are no rash statements to be found
in it, and no fanciful or extreme positions are assumed.
While not ignoring Christian experience touching
the presence and influence of the Spirit in individual
believers, the author observes on this profound and
mysterious point a commendable reserve, and speaks
with the hesitancy that must ever become the reverent
inquirer in this field. And this is praiseworthy; for
after all, blessed as Christian experience is, it is not
nor can be the ultimate court of appeal in deter-
mining the divine action of the Spirit, nor can
general deductions be drawn therefrom as to how
he operates and why. Our Lord spoke a very profound word, when, speaking of the Comforter, He
said, "He shall not speak from Himself; He shall
glorify Me." Rarely does the Spirit invite our
attention to His own presence and work in the soul;

rather, He uniformly turns our thoughts and affections to the Lord Jesus, the object of our faith, the center and sum of our hope. We have long been convinced that to study the presence and work of the Spirit in the believer apart from the Word is a mistake if not a perilous experiment. Even His witness with our spirit that we are the children of God (Rom. VIII: 16) is not apart from the Word, nor yet from the glory of Christ in whom alone we are brought into the filial relation (Jno. 1: 12.) Scripture holds the supreme place, and the author of this book uniformally turns to it for light and guidance.

Another thing is, these studies are reverential. There is everywhere manifest complete subjection to the authority of Scripture, and confidence in its unerring teaching. This is refreshing, particularly in these degenerate times, when too many, alas, seem disposed to sit in judgment on the Word, or bend it into conformity with their theories and presuppositions. Loyalty to God's truth is fast becoming the burning question of our day, even among evangelical churches. Because of its un-questioning loyalty, this book will prove helpful and stimulating.

Still another interesting feature of it is, its excellent bibliography. Most of that which has been published on the Holy Spirit since John Owen's book* finds a place in this well-selected list.

That God may use these studies relating to the person and work of His Divine Spirit for the further-ance of His cause and the good of His people is the prayer of the writer.

Xenia Theological Seminary   WILLIAM G. MOOREHEAD

*Reprinted as *The Holy Spirit: His Gifts and Power*
  by Kregel Publications, 1977.

PREFACE

THIS book is the outgrowth of the writer's own perplexity. This age is the dispensation of the third Person of the Trinity. For nineteen hundred years we have been saying, "I believe in the Holy Ghost," but how much do we believe in Him, and what is it we believe about Him? The method of His operation must forever remain an inscrutable mystery to finite minds, and subtle metaphysical distinctions are as useless here as they are presumptuous; but when once we realize that every relationship to the Father and the Son is brought about, and every treasure of their infinite love is made over to us through that operation, it will not seem strange that such great emphasis should be laid upon the necessity of an appreciation of what those relationships and treasures are in order to His Presence and power within us, such as God's plan for our Christian experience involves.

The surprising thing is, that this emphasis has been so long delayed; indeed, the past nineteen years have seen more literature on this subject issue from the press than all the rest of the nineteen hundred together. The "Bibliotheca" for forty-six years from the date of its first publication, 1844, contains not one article on the Holy Spirit; for more than forty years, from 1839, the "Methodist Quarterly" contained but one article; the "Princeton Review," in fifty-six years, from 1838, only one, and the same thing is true of all other theological magazines. Dr.

Charles Hodge gave us three ponderous volumes of
Systematic Theology, containing two thousand and
three hundred pages, and of this number only twelve
pages were devoted to the subject of the Holy Spirit;
and here, as well as in all other such literature, the
question, as a matter of course, has been treated
wholly as a theological dogma, with but little meaning
for the life and experience of the believer.

Surely in this day of spiritism, this emphasis upon
the relationship to the human soul of the Spirit, who
is to "guide into all truth," is timely and fortunate.
Would we but be guided by His gentle whisperings,
what absurdities of belief and denials of Him of
whom He came to witness might be spared. Yet not
alone for this, but for what it is the privilege and the
duty of a Spirit-indwelt man to be and do, is not
this revival of interest in the teaching of the Scriptures
concerning the Person and work of the Holy Spirit
of God and of His Son Christ Jesus a matter of great
rejoicing?

It is hoped this little volume will commend itself,
not as an earlier or later view simply clothed in new
language, nor yet as another opinion on this so vitally
important subject; human opinion is a worthless
thing if only Scripture hath spoken plainly. Nor has
it been meant in any way as controversial. The writer
in his own anxiety to appreciate his privilege as a
child of the Almighty has been left in confusion and
uncertainty by at least seemingly contradictory statements of different teachers upon the relationship of
this blessed Spirit of God to His children. For
instance, when Dr. James Gray ("The Holy Spirit
and the Believer," page 16), says, "The filling of the
Spirit is for holiness," and Dr. Torrey ("The
Baptism of the Holy Ghost," page 6) says, "The

baptism of the Spirit has nothing to do directly with cleansing from sin, but is connected with service," and when Dr. Gray (same page) says, "The anointing is for service," and Campbell Morgan ("Spirit of God," page 194) says, "The anointing which is on the child of God is that which was received at regeneration, and is not an experience after such a time," and when Dr. Chapman ("Received ye the Holy Ghost," page 75) says, "It is unscriptural for the Christian to be talking about the baptism of the Holy Ghost," and MacNeil ("Spirit-filled Life," page 38) says, "It surely cannot be unscriptural for a believer to pray, 'Lord Jesus, baptise me with the Holy Ghost;'" when these and many other such statements of apparent contradiction confront us we wonder whether the brethren are disagreeing about experiences which are vitally important to every earnest child of God, or whether it is merely a difference in nomenclature which amounts to nothing; and we have longed for some one to bring harmony, if possible, out of this apparent confusion. It is with this in view the writer has gone into a careful and, he hopes, an impartial exegesis of every passage in the Old and New Scriptures where mention is made of the Holy Spirit. It is his earnest desire that these pages be received in the spirit they have been produced, not as a challenge to any man's teaching, but as a sincere effort to get such teaching before us alongside the Word of God in such a way that the earnest inquirer may come out of what to many has been a state of perplexity, to an appreciation of his spiritual privilege such as will commend itself to his own soul.

To this end and that the student may gain a comprehensive view of the present-day teaching, this teaching has been taken in quotation from the various volumes, the exact reference being noted in each instance by the page where it is written, and when alongside has been brought all of such Scripture as will bear upon the teaching in question, an endeavour has been made to help the reader to what we believe should commend itself to him as a safe and impartial explanation of such Scripture, and consequently the Scriptural way of viewing the matter under consideration.

The multiplication of words has been studiously avoided; little thought is paid to style, other than to make it too plain for any misconstruction to be placed upon its meaning. A Bibliography has been added for those wishing to prosecute more thoroughly this important study.

With earnest prayer that the blessing of Him of whom it so unworthily speaks, may rest upon this humble effort to the edification and comfort of those in whom He dwells, it is sent forth upon its mission.

WILLIAM E. BIEDERWOLF

STUDY OF THE HOLY SPIRIT

1

THE NAME OF THE HOLY SPIRIT

In the Old Testament are found ninety distinct references to the Holy Spirit, among which are eighteen different designations; in the New Testament, two hundred and sixty-four references and thirty-nine different designations; five of these are common to both, thus leaving fifty-two designations in the entire Word; expressive of His relation to God, seventeen; to the Son, five; to man, nineteen; of His own character, seven, and of His essential deity, five. For an exhaustive tabulation of these designations see Macgregor, "Things of the Spirit," page 17, or Cumming, "Through the Eternal Spirit," page 48. In the above fifty-two instances, four times He is called the Comforter, forty-three times the Spirit, in some one of His relations, the remaining five being descriptive phrases of the same Person. We have then two names applied to the third Person of the Trinity, namely, the Holy Spirit and the Comforter.

"Spiritus" is the Latin word synonymous with the Greek word "Pneuma," both literally signifying "breath" or "wind." As applied to the Divine essence there can be no allusion to their original meaning, which is but the imagery representative of the Holy Spirit's presence and approach to men. The Holy Spirit is called the "breath of God" with reference to His mode of subsistence, proceeding from God as the breath from the mouth. Notice the characteristic action of Jesus in John 20: 22. In referring to the breath or spirit of man the old English used the word "ghost,"—giving up the ghost; and so of the breath of God was used the expression "Holy Ghost," and while the weird associations of the word ghost in its present-day signification are all forgotten when this blessed Personality is so designated, yet since the Latin "Spirit" has so truly become a part of the English language it would seem to be the more preferable designation of the two, which the American Revised Version has accordingly adopted. The Holy Spirit is not therefore called Spirit on account of the spirituality of His essence, for this is likewise to be predicted of the Father and of the Son. Neither is He called Holy with reference to the holiness of His nature, for He is no more so than either of the other Persons of the Trinity; it has reference to His official character; He is the author of all holiness.

The other designation of this Holy Personage is the "Comforter," so called four times by Jesus in His farewell discourse, John 14: 16, 26; 15: 26, and 16: 7. This is the only single appellation suggestive of the Spirit's character and work. The Greek word is "Parakletos." Given by Jesus as descriptive of "another" one like Himself, rich in meaning as is the word itself, as a name for this divine Person whose relation to the Christian is so intimate, it ought to commend itself strongly and tenderly to the heart of every child of God. Because no word in the English language can furnish us with a translation co-extensive with the infinite stretches of meaning in this word Paraclete, why, instead of crippling it with inadequate translations, is it not better to Anglicize it into Paraclete and so retain it both in Scripture and in usage?

The same word in I John 2: 1, referring to Christ, is translated "Advocate," and Meyer, Godet, Westcott and many others so translate it in the Gospel, while Alford, Schaff and as many others retain the translation "Comforter." Philologically "parakletos" can no more be rendered "comforter" than can "kletos" be rendered "caller"; this last must be "called," and, therefore, "parakletos," "called to aid"; hence advocate, which accords with Greek usage where friends or agents stood before the judge to plead the cause of another.

The verb from which it comes is always, save in Acts 28: 20, used in the sense of "to comfort," but this active sense is easily contained in the idea of an advocate as involved in the passive "called to aid." An advocate is one who stands by (Beistand-DeWette), not only as an intercessor but as a helper, comforter and consoler. Futhermore, the noun was evidently imported irrespective of its derivation from the then current judicial phraseology, and this observation has all the more weight, inasmuch as John, the only one who uses the noun Parakletos, is precisely the one who never uses the verb from which it is derived, and which is elsewhere so common in the New Testament. To this add the express use of "Advocate" in I John 2: 1, and it would seem that such must have been the idea in the mind of Jesus as interpreted by John.

Hence, if the word Paraclete is not to be retained, then of the two translations under consideration, "Advocate" as the more grammatical and the more inclusive should be given preference; but it must be remembered that comforting and aiding is an important part of a real advocate's work; yet as the thought of pleading is so prominently and almost exclusively associated with the word advocate in this day we are more than ever impressed with the wisdom of retaining the original word Paraclete,—called to aid.

How much they would need such an one; Jesus had indeed been a Paraclete unto them. One upon whom they had leaned in every perplexity and trial; but now He was going away; welcome indeed then must have been His words falling in rich promise upon their waiting hearts. They were not to be deserted, but "another" Paraclete, such an one as Jesus was and yet another, was to come; indeed the Coming One was to be no other than Christ Himself —"I will not leave you orphans; I will come unto you." Not only was the Paraclete to take the place of the Christ they knew and loved and leaned upon in human form, but in His coming was to be returned to them in presence invisible their then exalted and glorified Friend by whose loss they were now about to be bereaved.

2

THE ADVENT OF THE HOLY SPIRIT

THE Holy Spirit has ever been omnipresent, but He is here to-day in a sense which was not always true of Him. Three distinct periods of His operation are witnessed in the Word.

I. From creation to Christ; He shared the creative work, Gen. 1: 2. He came upon men in the Old Testament, I Sam. 10: 6; He entered into them, Ez. 2: 2; He filled them, Ex. 28: 3; He strove with men, Gen. 6: 3, and spoke to them, Ezk. 2: 2.

II. From Christ to Pentecost. He filled John the Baptist, Luke 1: 15; Elizabeth, Luke 1: 41; Zacharias, Luke 1: 67, and the Saviour. The Saviour

(a) Was conceived by the Holy Spirit, Matt. 1: 18, 20; Lu. 1: 35.

(b) Was anointed by the Holy Spirit, Matt. 3: 16, 17; Mk. 1: 10, 11; Lu. 3: 21, 22; 4: 18; and John 1: 32, 33.

(c) Was led by the Holy Spirit, Matt. 4: 1; Mk. 1: 12; Lu. 4:1.

(d) Was taught by the Holy Spirit, Acts 1: 2; John 14: 10, 24.

(e) Wrought miracles by the Holy Spirit, Matt. 12: 28; Lu. 11: 20.

(f) Offered Himself up through the Holy Spirit, Heb. 9: 14.

(g) Was raised by the Holy Spirit, Rom. 8:
    11 and 1: 4.

III.   From Pentecost to Parousia. Pentecost has
been called by Augustine the "dies natalis" of the
Holy Spirit. That the Holy Spirit came to us in
this world shortly after the Saviour's ascension in a
new and permanent capacity, the words of John 7:
39, make evident, which coming was in fulfillment
both of Old Testament prophecy, Joel 2: 28, with
Acts 2: 39, and of the Saviour's promise in John 14:
16 and 15: 26. See also Acts 2: 33. In one sense
always here, but in another His abode before Pentecost was with the Father. Strictly speaking, there
can be no localization of an omnipresent being since
His omnipresence relates to His essence and His
comings and goings are accommodations to finite
conception.

The chief differences between His relation to the
first and third periods designated are:

1. In the first He came occasionally. "A
   transient visitor"—Augustine; in the third
   He came to "abide" forever, John 14: 16.
2. In the first He equipped a few men for the
   accomplishment of a special work; in the
   third He offers Himself in fulness to all,
   Acts 2: 39.
       Notice also that in the first He was not
   revealed to the saints as a personality
   distinct from God; God was known and
   worshipped in His unity; the Trinity
   though implied was not clearly revealed.

The time of the Spirit's coming to take up His
permanent abode in the church was fifty days after

the Saviour's resurrection, and called Pentecost, which in itself has no suggestion of fulness or out-pouring, but is simply a designation of time meaning "fiftieth." The entire arrangement was definitely foreshadowed in Old Testament rites, Lev. 23: 11–16.

I. The slaying of the paschal lamb typified the sacrifice of the Saviour foretelling the day of its occurrence.

II. "On the morrow after the Sabbath" was the sheaf of first fruits to be waved before the Lord, foretelling the resurrection on the first day of the week.

III. Then "seven Sabbaths shall be completed even unto the morrow after the seventh Sabbath shall ye number fifty days," foretelling the time of the Spirit's advent.

The disciples were told to tarry, Luke 24: 49, and they would be filled with the Spirit; they tarried ten days and the filling came. How often are they repre-sented as wondering during these ten days why the filling did not come, and possibly they did; but when it is said it was a waiting consequent upon the necessity of their first being emptied, we lose sight altogether of the dispensational character of the arrangement. They waited ten days for no other reason save that it was yet ten days until the fiftieth day would come. If the disciples did not at first divine this, as the days passed without the promise fulfilled, it would certainly have dawned upon them as the fiftieth day drew near.

I. The time of the Spirit's advent was determined by the Saviour's glorification, John 7: 39, and this finds explanation in that the office of the Spirit is to communicate to the church and to realize in the church the benefits of Christ's work, and only when this work was completed, when He had died for our sins, risen again for our justification, ascended to glory, there to be our Intercessor with the Father, —only then could the Holy Spirit have a finished image to complete in the soul. "The Divine Artist could not fitly descend to make the copy before the original had been provided."—Archer Butler.

II. Pentecost inaugurated the mystical Church of Christ. The disciples who followed Jesus were no longer a mere number of individuals concurring in sentiment concerning their Master, but were merged into a living vital unity, a temple indwelt of God through the Spirit, Eph. 2: 21, 22; I Cor. 3: 16.

III. Pentecost was the Installation day of the Holy Spirit as Administrator of the affairs of the church "until He come."

IV. Pentecost can no more be repeated than can Bethlehem, Calvary, or the resurrection.

THE PERSONALITY OF THE HOLY SPIRIT

Is the Holy Spirit an influence, a virtue, an emanation from or manifestation of the divine, a mere impersonal force, or is the Holy Spirit a person intelligent and active? That the latter is true and not the former the following considerations will make apparent.

I. The essential parts of personality are four: Understanding, will, affection and appreciation of the moral. All these are predicated of the Holy Spirit.

    (a) He is said to know the things of God, I Cor. 2: 10, 11.

    (b) He distributes His gifts to every man as He will, I Cor. 12: 11.

    (c) He loves and may be grieved, II Tim. 1: 7 and Eph. 4: 30.

        (On the Love of the Spirit, see Cumming, "Through the Eternal Spirit," page 175.)

    (d) He reproves of sin, Jno. 16: 9, and guides into truth, John 16: 13.

II. Functions not ascribable to an influence, or to aught save a person are attributed to the Holy Spirit. He hears, John 16: 13. He speaks, Acts 10: 19; 13: 2, 8; 8: 29; John 16: 13; Mark 13: 11;

Heb. 3: 7. He prays, Rom. 8: 26. He teaches, Luke 12: 12; John 14: 26. He forbids, Acts 16: 6, 7. He comforts, Acts 9: 31. He guides, John 16: 13. He reveals, John 16: 14, 15; Luke 2: 26. He witnesses, Rom. 8: 16. He strives with men, Gen. 6: 3. He quickens the memory, John 14: 26. He performs miracles, Acts 2: 4; 8: 39. He calls to the ministry, Acts 13: 2, and sets pastors over churches, Acts 20: 28.

III. Men sustain relations toward the Holy Spirit such as are possible only toward a person. They grieve Him, Eph. 4: 30; they resist Him, Acts 7: 51; they sin against Him, Matt. 12: 31; Mark 3: 29; they invoke His communion, II Cor. 13: 14; they are baptized into His name, Matt. 28: 19; they lie to Him, Acts 5: 3; they rebel against Him, Isa. 63: 10; they insult Him, Heb. 10: 29.

IV. The name given to the Holy Spirit and the pronouns used in reference to Him are distinct proofs of His personality.

> (a) Jesus calls Him Paraclete, or one who comforts or stands by to aid.
> (b) Jesus uses the masculine pronoun, "When He, the Spirit, is come, He," etc. Even in John 14: 26, where the neuter relative agrees with the noun Spirit, the following pronoun, which naturally would be neuter, is masculine.

V. That the Holy Spirit is a personality distinct from the Father and the Son is evident from the fact that He is said to be the Spirit of God, Matt. 3: 16; I Cor. 6: 11; II Cor. 3: 3; I Peter 4: 14; and the Spirit of Christ, Rom. 8: 9; Phil. 1: 19; Acts 16: 7. He proceedeth from God, John 16: 26;

He is sent by the Father, John' 14: 26, and by the Son, John 15: 26. They could not send themselves. Jesus says He will send another Paraclete, namely, one distinct from Himself, and in Romans 8: 26, the Spirit is said to make intercession; certainly the Father could not make intercession to Himself. How the idea of the Holy Spirit as a distinct personality could be more clearly set forth than is done in the Word of God is impossible for an unbiased mind to conceive.

THE DEITY OF THE HOLY SPIRIT

THE names of Divinity are ascribed to Him. In Isa. 6: 8, Isaiah says, "I heard the voice of Jehovah saying, etc." In Acts 28: 25, 26, Paul, quoting the passage, says, "Well spake the Holy Spirit by Isaiah." In Jer. 31: 31, it is said, "Behold the days come saith Jehovah, etc." In Heb. 10: 15, it is said, referring to the same passage, "The Holy Spirit after that He said, etc." In Acts 5: 4, He is expressly called God. Peter said Satan had inspired Ananias to lie to the Holy Spirit, and then he added, "Thou hast not lied unto men but unto God." See also II Cor. 3: 17, 18 (A. R. V.), where He is called the Lord. See also Eph. 2: 22; I Cor. 6: 19; Rom. 8: 9, 10.

II. The perfections of Divinity are ascribed to the Holy Spirit. The attributes of God are the attributes of the Holy Spirit.

(a) Eternity, Heb. 9: 14. Unto Him as unto Jehovah can the lofty praise of Ps. 90: 2, be ascribed.

(b) Omniscience, I Cor. 2: 10, 11; Isa. 40: 13.

(c) Omnipotence, Micah 3: 8. Proven by His works. (See III.)

(d) Omnipresence, Ps. 139: 7, 10. Same idea in reference to God, Jer. 23: 24.

III.   The works of Divinity are ascribed to the Holy Spirit.

    (a)   The work of creation is His. Gen. 1: 2; Job 26: 13; Ps. 33: 6; Job 33: 4.

    (b)   The work of providence is His, Ps. 104: 30.

    (c)   The work of regeneration and resurrection are His, John 3: 5, and Rom. 8: 11. He is in fact the source of the miraculous, Matt. 12: 28; I Cor. 12: 9, 11.

IV.   The worship of Divinity is given to Him.

    (a)   We are baptized into the name of the Holy Spirit as well as that of the Father and the Son, thus setting forth an equality of dignity among the three.

    (b)   Seven times in Rev. obedience to His admonition is enjoined upon us.

    (c)   While there is no mention of direct prayer to Him it is involved in His name (Paraclete—one called to aid) and also in the Apostolic benediction, II Cor. 13: 14, and the invocation of John, Rev. 1: 4, 5.

    (d)   He may be sinned against—in fact the only sin that can never be pardoned is directed against the Holy Spirit, Matt. 12: 31, 32, in view of which His Godhead must certainly be recognized.

THE SEALING OF THE HOLY SPIRIT

THE idea of a seal is twofold, that of authentication and ownership or security. In John 6: 27, God's seal upon Christ is made to consist in the miracles wrought by Christ through the power of the Spirit given to Him without measure,—that is authentication.

In Eph. 1: 13, believers are sealed with the promised Spirit, promised by God through Joel.

Every genuine believer is sealed. The sealing is "next after faith," says Prof. Smeaton. Logically and theologically this is true, but chronologically they are practically simultaneous,—"upon believing we are sealed." Believing is essential to and the foundation of sealing. The literal reading of Eph. 1: 13, is "having believed," not "after that ye believed,—ye were sealed." Campbell Morgan is therefore right when he says, "*The Sealing of the Spirit is identical with regeneration,*" ("Spirit of God," page 192.) He in fact makes it identical with the baptism of the Spirit, but in his mind this last is the same with regeneration.

Moule refers the sealing to such experiences as Acts 8: 17 and 10: 44. MacNeil ("Spirit-filled Life," page 45), says it is the same as the baptism of the Spirit, by which he means a definite post-regenerative experience, and that Paul in Eph. 1: 13, had in mind the incident of Acts 19: 1–7, which, however, is altogether gratuitous. Gordon, ("Ministry of the Spirit," pages 88 and 99), and Cumming, ("Through the Eternal Spirit," page 112), have likewise so construed its meaning. Each of these last three writers conceives of the Filling of the Spirit and the Baptism of the Spirit and the Enduement of the Spirit as a later experience than regeneration, and make these and the sealing equivalent to one and the same thing; and unless Dr. John Owen, who has written so exhaustively on this subject ("Discourse Concerning the Spirit," pages 406, 407), is to be quoted in support of the same position, his language at this point is not without ambiguity; all of which is very surprising.

Such experiences as the above mentioned are seals in the sense of God's approval and confirmation, but either to thus limit the idea of a seal or to make such its primal reference is grammatically out of harmony with every New Testament passage which refers to the believer's sealing, as well as the only reference it can possibly bear so far as the idea of ownership and security is involved in the word, which idea in this passage, Eph. 1: 13, as in others similar to it, is God's ownership and securing of His people—of all believers. So teach Meyer, Ellicott, Hodge, Riddle and Smeaton. Of course God demands holiness, II Tim. 2: 19, but it is faith that saves, and to make God's ownership depend on the filling of the Spirit is to make it, according to the construction of those with whom we are now taking issue, depend on something subsequent to regeneration. It is sad that all Christians are not filled with the Spirit; it would be sadder still to think that all who are not thus filled will be disowned in the day of redemption "unto" which we are sealed. See Eph. 4: 30. *Every Christian is sealed and has the "earnest of the Spirit," which is the Spirit Himself.*

There is one other passage, II Cor. 1: 21, 22, "Now he which establisheth us with you in Christ and hath anointed us is God, who hath also sealed us and given the earnest of the Spirit in our hearts." Here Hodge, Olshausen, Smeaton and others refer the "us" in the two last instances not alone to Paul and Timothy, but to all Christians as well. Meyer and Lange say, Paul designedly distinguishes between "us with you" and "us," and referred the anointing and sealing to teachers only; they, however, admit that even their interpretation would not deny the anointing and sealing to all believers, and quote Eph. 1: 13, and 4: 30, in substantiation. Yes, *every child of God is sealed*, and at the coming of the Lord He shall know us by the sign we bear.

"The allusion to the seal as a pledge of purchase would be peculiarly intelligible to the Ephesians, for Ephesus was a maritime city and an extensive trade in timber was carried on there by the ship masters of the neighboring ports. The method of purchase was this: The merchant, after selecting his timber, stamped it with his own signet, which was an acknowledged sign of ownership. He often did not carry off his possession at the time; it was left in the harbor with other floats of timber; but it was chosen, bought and stamped, and in due time the merchant sent a trusty agent with the signet, who, finding that timber which bore a corresponding impress, claimed and brought it away for the master's use. Thus the Holy Spirit impresses on the soul now the image of Jesus Christ and this is the sure pledge of everlasting inheritance." Bickersteth,—"The Spirit of Life."

6

THE ANOINTING OF THE HOLY SPIRIT

In Luke 4: 18, Jesus says He was "anointed," doubtless referring to His experience at baptism, and in Acts 4: 27, and 10: 38, the same thing is referred to. In the Old Testament priests, prophets and kings were anointed to signify their separation and consecration to office, and the passages above referred to contain the same idea. The Anointing, as the Seal, is the Holy Spirit.

Jesus was conceived by the Spirit, Luke 1: 35, and like John the Baptist, was certainly filled with the Spirit from His mother's womb. As a child we know he was filled, Luke 2: 40. The reception of the Holy Spirit at His Incarnation may certainly with propriety be called His first anointing, and may in a sense be considered as His only one. While as regards the baptismal anointing the immediate connection and reference is to the manifest and visible resting upon Jesus of the Spirit at His baptism, yet it is not to be thought of as implying another and distinct reception of the Spirit, but the rather that the Spirit already in Him in fulness manifested Himself in a way annunciatory of Christ's official capacity. Smeaton, page 21, speaks of three degrees in Christ's anointing: at Incarnation, at Baptism and at Glorification.

"In the New Testament," says Hodge, "official

anointing is spoken of only in relation to Christ
and never in relation to the Apostles or others."
This is true, unless II Cor. 1: 21, is an exception
and this we are not inclined to believe. Now in
I John 2: 20, the anointing is predicated of all
believers; so likewise in II Cor. 1: 21. There are
those who speak of receiving an anointing for each
particular service, (referring of course to a special
filling for such special work), but such a use of the
word anointing is without Scriptural warrant.
Others draw such inference from the supposed
analogy between Christ, the Anointed One, and
Christians, but this is, after all, a supposition which
receives no encouragement from the reasonable
inference of God's dealings with the perfect
pattern and its imperfect imitations. Morgan, page
194, has rightly said, "The anointing which is
on the child of God is that which was received
at regeneration."

Gordon says, "Sealing and anointing and enduement, (and by 'enduement,' he means the Baptism
of the Spirit which in his mind is the same with
the Filling of the Spirit) are one and the same
experience." But if the seal is the sign of ownership, then those without this seal or special enduement are not God's property and the question will
arise, how much of an enduement, of a filling, or
baptism of the Spirit must one have in order to
be owned? As priests and kings were anointed so
Christians receiving an anointing from the Holy
One in the moment of regeneration, are comformably
to Scripture (Rev. 1: 6; 5: 10), called "priests and
kings unto God"; but of this glory, according to
the idea now in review, all are deprived who are
without this special post-regenerative experience.

One Christian has or can have no more of an anointing than another; the anointing is the Holy Spirit, and the expression, "the same anointing teacheth you all things," is but a calling to remembrance of what the same writer had said in his Gospel, John 16: 13, "Howbeit when He the Spirit of truth is come He will guide you into all truth."

It is well to bear in mind, however, that although there is no Scriptural mention of the word anointing from which to draw a warrant for applying such a term to any experience of the believer apart from his regeneration, yet there can be no reasonable objection to the use of such a term in connection with a post-regenerative experience if only we are careful to distinguish what is meant by it. If the search be one of words, once regenerated, there is no other anointing; if it be one of experience, call it what you will so long as the above caution be observed. *The Holy Spirit taking up His abode in the individual seals him by that very act and also, according to Scriptural usage, anoints him; then once within He endues the soul with power according to the freedom given Him and the needs of the occasion. This it will shortly appear is the filling of the Spirit, but when that occasion is the going forth to service this preparation of the servant may with no impropriety, be called an anointing, if it be borne in mind that it is nothing other than the Spirit's filling for the special service at hand.*

7

THE COMMUNION OF THE HOLY SPIRIT

In II Cor. 13: 14, Paul invokes for the Corinthian Christians the "communion of the Holy Spirit." It is impossible to tell precisely what Paul meant by the word translated communion, and to be arbitrary or over-positive in the exposition of such Scripture is simply to set your mind against the minds of countless other scholars toward whom the impartial student must have respect. Not that we can wholly miss Paul's meaning, but that of the various shades of meaning belonging to any particular word it is not at all times possible to know just to which one the writer had reference. The Greek word is Koinonia and is in both versions translated "communion." It occurs in its various forms in the Septuagint fifteen times, and in the New Testament eighty-two times. Of the New Testament mention it is fifty-five times variously translated "communion," "fellowship," "participation," "communication," and twenty-seven times in the sense of "common" or "unclean." In three of the fifty-five instances it is the communion of a person, II Cor. 13: 14; Phil. 2: 1; I Cor. 1: 9. To these we wish to direct attention. The thought embodied in them, however, can more accurately be discovered after the following observations. The word is used in the following senses:

I. To be a partaker of a thing (I Tim. 5: 22, etc.), eleven times.

II. To be a participator in a thing (Phil. 4: 14, etc.), nine times.

In each instance there is a "with some person," understood fourteen times, expressed by the preposition "with" five times, and by "of them" once.

III. To have fellowship with a person (I John 1: 3, etc.), five times; in each case there is an "in something," understood four times, and mentioned once (Phil. 4: 15). In the first twenty (I, II) the thing in which was mentioned, and the person with whom understood; in the last five just the reverse; thus in all the twenty-five the thought is that of Koinonia *with* a person *in* a thing, and this same thought will, we believe, be seen to underlie every other use of the expression. II Cor. 6: 14, light (personified) having fellowship *with* darkness (personified), that is, *in* the deeds of darkness, Eph. 5: 11, fellowship,—*with* evil men or the Evil One or with darkness (personified), *in* unfruitful works.

IV. Five times it is a contribution, I Tim. 6: 18; Rom. 15: 26; 12: 13; Heb. 13: 16; I Cor. 9: 13.

V. Once it is a contributor. I Tim. 6: 18.

VI. Once it is the act of contributing, Gal. 6: 6.

In these last seven the same idea is involved— persons and things. What is fellowship but a union or communion of possessions? There can be no real communion without a sharing of what belongs to us whether it be a crust of bread, the interchange of thought, of affection or sympathy.

VII. Four times it is said they had a community of things, Acts 2: 44; 4: 32; Tit. 1: 4; Jude 3; the above applies likewise to these.

VIII. Twice it is to have a partner, II Cor. 8: 23; Phil. 17.

IX. Once it is to be a partner *with* someone, Luke 5: 10.

X. Twice it is to be a partner *of* someone, I Cor. 10: 20; Heb. 10: 33. What is the thought in these last five but sharers with each other,—hence fellowship, communion,—in something.

XI. Gal 2: 9, To share with them in the Gospel.

XII. I Cor. 10: 18, To be a partaker of the altar, that is, of the blessing for which the altar stood, through God's sharing such blessings with them or furnishing them to them, the result of which of course is communion with God by such partaking.

XIII. Acts 2: 42, Fellowship with each other in religious sympathies, service, community of goods, etc.

XIV. Phil. 6, A difficult passage, "The faith which you have in common with the rest of us," being possibly the best of many explanations, in which case it would belong to those references of "a community of things." On any of the proposed explanations, however, it is in harmony with the general idea which we have seen to be resident in the expression, Koinonia *with* someone *in* something.

Now to the three passages in question. An explanation of one will suffice for all. In II Cor. 13: 14, Paul invokes for them the "*communion of the Holy Spirit.*" Notice it does not say with the Holy Spirit, although the force of the preposition we feel has been unduly pressed, for in I Cor. 1: 9, we read that we are called into the fellowship *of* the Son, and in I John 1: 3, it is said our fellowship is *with* the Son. There

is a distinction, but the ideas are interdependent, and
to press the "of" relation to the exclusion of the
"with" relation in the passage under consideration
is hardly in keeping with impartial exegesis. Dr.
Cumming, (Through the Eternal Spirit,—page 185),
adheres to the usually accepted meaning of commun-
ing or having fellowship with the Holy Spirit Himself. This thought of special intimacy with the Third
Person of the Trinity is certainly very attractive and
is in keeping with the general tenor of Scripture.
It is, however, nowhere explicitly taught, and though
involved in what Paul here says, can hardly be considered the primary idea.

Now the eleven instances where "of" is used all
contain the idea of "participation in," and owing
to such analogy it is impossible to dispute with
Meyer, Lange, Riddle, who here make the meaning
"participation in the Holy Spirit," but in the eleven
instances mentioned the participation is in a thing;
here Paul speaks of a person, and as the preposition
"of" in this clause is of precisely the same grammatical force as the "of" in the other two clauses of
the verse, the grace of Christ and the love of God
being the grace and love of which they are the authors,
so in the third clause it seems proper to make the
Koinonia that of which the Holy Spirit is the author,
namely, the spiritual riches which He furnishes. To
the above reasons we may add that as we have already
seen and as all authority admits, such rendering is
not in the least at variance with the linguistic usage
of the word itself.

In this pregnant truth there is involved a threefold relationship which may in order be expressed as
the "of" relation, the "in" relation, and the "with"
relation, any one of which must by the very nature of

the idea include all the others. The "of" relation, the one of chief emphasis here, refers to Koinonia as the spiritual riches communicated, that is, communications; the "in" relation refers to our participation in the things communicated, and the "with" relation to the communion (fellowship) with the Holy Spirit Himself in such participation, the whole of which of course proceeds upon the supposition of a previous participation in the Holy Spirit as the basic principle of all spiritual Koinonia.

As before mentioned, fellowship with a person is impossible save through a participation in something which has become a common possession through the gift of one or the other or mutually of both, and as one thus participates he can but have communion with the furnisher of the blessings at his disposal.

What a depth of meaning to the word when thus construed; all the inexhaustible treasures that are hid in Christ, the very fulness of God Himself to be ours through the Holy Spirit, the Great Communicator, beginning with the very life that regenerates and ending with the glory that transfigures. There came from the press some years ago a strange book representing a man who had lived through a trance to a period a hundred years after it came upon him. Society had made marvelous advances and everywhere the man turned he was met with new revelations of grandeur and glory; they were so many it took him months to comprehend them all, and oftentimes he would sit down to contemplate and to wonder at the marvelous things to which he had fallen heir. It is so with the study of the Holy Spirit. At every step we find some new treasure, some rich experience, to which we have become heirs through the "communion of the Holy Spirit," until long before we have comprehended the half of our inheritance we are simply compelled to sit and wonder how it ever could be so. What are some of these treasures, these communications? Paul in another place has referred to them as "the fruit of the Spirit," and this chapter may properly be completed in another.

8

THE FRUITS OF THE HOLY SPIRIT

In the few pages immediately following will be found the results of a careful effort to count up our treasures which are hid for us in Christ and made over to us through the Communion of the Holy Spirit. To have these things in overflowing abundance is the privilege of the Spirit-filled believer. How rich that heritage is may the following summary help us to appreciate. Of these graces, these communications, all of which are the fruit of the Spirit, we find distinct mention of no less than fifty-seven.

I.   In Gal. 5: 22, Paul enumerates the following:

    (a) Love,—general inner disposition.
    (b) Joy,—because conscious of divine love.
    (c) Peace,—inner tranquility.
    (d) Long-suffering,—patience under trial.
    (e) Kindness,—kindly disposed to others.
    (f) Goodness,—beneficence, kindness in action.
    (g) Faithfulness,—fidelity, trustworthiness.
    (h) Meekness,—mildness and submissiveness.
    (i) Temperance,—self-control.

II.   Peter also has a list, faith being presupposed as a foundation upon which they must rest, II Peter 1: 5–8.

    (a) Diligence,—earnest use of energies.
    (b) Virtue,—manly courageousness in conduct.

(c) Knowledge,—recognition of the dutiful and appropriate.

(d) Temperance,—self-control.

(e) Patience,—perseverance in abuse and temptation.

(f) Godliness,—reverence for God and action accordingly.

(g) Love of brethren,—that is, of Christians.

(h) Love for all.

This list differs in arrangement and constituents from Paul's. Paul begins with love; Peter ends with it. Paul begins with love as the spring of all other graces because he is drawing a picture of the spiritual character in contrast to the works of the flesh. Peter is concerned here with the growth of spiritual character and so presupposes faith as the foundation upon which by means of these varied virtues the superstructure is reared.

The fruit of the Spirit as mentioned elsewhere.

I. Faith.

(a) I Cor. 12: 3, "Calling Jesus Lord by the Spirit," that is, justifying, saving faith.

(b) II Cor. 4: 13, Spirit of faith, referring not so much here to justifying faith as to confidence in God in the midst of affliction.

(c) I Cor. 12: 9, Gift of faith—a high degree of the ordinary grace, especially for miraculous manifestation; this seems to have been a gift designed especially and probably only for the early church.

II.   Regeneration.

(a) John 3: 5, 6, Born of the Spirit.
(b) Titus 3: 5, Renewing by the Spirit. Lange
     refers this to a continued process, and
     while the word in itself so means, yet in
     this case the thought in question and the
     past tense of the verb "saved" (Meyer
     and Riddle) best refer it to the renewing
     of the soul at regeneration.

III.   Spiritual life. John 6: 63, the originator
and supplier; also Rom. 8: 2. Rom. 8: 6, in fulness
now and of course hereafter where it culminates
in the perfect life.

IV.   Self-dedication to God. I Cor. 6: 11. The
word "sanctify" is in the middle voice and not the
passive, as the Revised Version makes it, and denotes
properly the setting apart of oneself as holy unto God.

V.   Sanctification.

(a) I Cor. 6: 11, Washed by the Spirit; the
     verb is middle and hence indicates our
     own effort united with that of the Spirit.
(b) I Cor. 6: 11, Made righteous by the Spirit;
     this seems a solitary use of this verb in this
     sense; it is the verb's simplest sense. Most
     retain the usual sense of "declare just," but
     the order hardly permits this. (See Meyer.)
(c) I Peter 1: 2, and II Thes. 2: 13, In the
     sanctification of the Spirit. Whether
     this word denotes the process or the
     result of the Spirit's working it is in
     either case a fruit of the Spirit. It is
     the sphere in which our election and
     choice to salvation is realized.

(d) II Cor. 3: 18, Growth into the Christ image.

(e) Rom. 14: 17, Righteousness, that is, inner, Meyer, Godet; Lange, Hodge, Moule, say imputed. The former is favored by the context, by the practical nature of the discourse and by verses 16, 18, 19, and also by the primary meaning of the word. Paul's general usage favors the second view. See also Rom. 8: 4.

(f) Rom. 15: 16, Sanctified by the Holy Spirit.

VI. Victory over sin.

(a) Gal. 5: 17; also Rom. 8: 2, if this refers to sanctification, which we are inclined to believe, though Dr. Hodge opposes such reference.

(b) Rom. 8: 13, Mortifying the deeds of the body through the Spirit.

VII. New power for spiritual conflict. Eph. 6: 10.

VIII. Likeness to Christ. Eph. 3: 19, "filled with all the fulness of God" which is contained in Christ (Col. 1: 19, and 2: 9). Though not called a fruit of the Spirit, one cannot analyze the prayer in Eph. 3: 16–19, without seeing that such is the evident result of being strengthened through the Spirit. As Christ in Col. 1: 19, is said to contain all the pleroma of God, so here such is the prayer for us, the pleroma being that with which God is filled,—the divine perfections; and notice he says *all* the pleroma,—His love, His knowledge, His power, His goodness, His holiness, etc.

IX.   Knowledge of divine truth. I Cor. 2: 10, 14.

(a) Eph. 1: 17, "Wisdom" here refers to a general continued condition of illumination and "revelation," to an advance on wisdom, that is, the more special gift of insight.

(b) John 16: 13, "Into all truth,"—full knowledge of the truth as it is in Christ; the whole truth of God.

(c) John 14: 26, "Teach all things," referring to a right and complete understanding of the truth as it is in Christ.

(d) I Cor. 2: 15, "All things,"—pre-eminently the deep things of God, verse 10, with a probable secondary reference to the affairs of life, that is, judgment and discretion in daily duty, etc.

The following seems to have been limited to special agents,—Apostolic.

(a) John 16: 13, "Things to come," referring not alone to eschatological revelations, but to the whole career of the church militant after the Spirit's coming. The destiny of the church.

(b) Eph. 3: 3, 5, The purpose of God as it is in Christ with a probable primal reference to the inclusion of the Gentiles.

(c) I Peter 1: 11, 12, Christ in them as the Revealer.

Examples—Acts 11: 28, Agabus prophesying.
  Acts 13: 2, Told to appoint to office; same idea in 20: 28.

Acts 20: 23, Revealed coming afflictions to Paul.
Acts 21: 4, Revealed coming afflictions to disciples.
Acts 21: 11, Revealed coming afflictions to Agabus.

X.   Assurance of Sonship.   Gal. 4: 6,—here the
Holy Spirit cries; Rom. 8: 15,—here the human
spirit cries; the idea is the same, because as Meyer
says, "The Spirit is so completely the author of the
Abba invocation that the man who invokes appears
only as the organ of the Spirit." Here also belong
Rom. 8: 16; Eph. 1: 13; 4: 30; II Cor. 1: 21, 22.

XI.   Led by the Spirit.   Gal. 5: 18; also Rom.
8: 14, 1, 4.

(a)   Gal. 5: 16, Walking about in the midst of
daily duties.

(b)   Gal. 5: 25, A careful, studied walk, being
the use of a different verb from 5: 16.

(c)   Inward intimation, Acts 8: 29; 11: 12;
13: 4; also Acts 16: 6, 7.
Some, Cumming, (Through the Eternal
Spirit, page 196) notice a shade of meaning between the "forbid" of vs. 6 and
the "suffer not" of vs. 7, the latter
leading of the Spirit not being so clear;
the first would not allow them, the
second simply gave no permission.

(d)   Acts 19: 21, Purposed in the Spirit,—the
Holy Spirit, Gloag, Cumming; his own
spirit, Meyer, Riddle, Hackett, R.V. Even
in the latter case it would be under the
impulse of the Holy Spirit.

(e)   Acts 16: 9, Led by a vision—the call to
Macedonia, 23: 11,—the visit to Rome
confirmed; Acts 10, Led up to pray, that
is, given a vision and told to go.

(f) II Cor. 12: 18, Guided by the Spirit. Simeon led by the Spirit, Lu. 2: 27. Jesus, Lu. 4: 1, "led." The Holy Spirit, His ruling and guiding principle, induced Him to go, acting on His soul for that purpose; (en, with the dative). Matt. 4: 1, "Led up,"—the external idea more emphasized. Actual guidance, (hupo, with the genitive). Mk. 1: 12, "Driveth," —cast out; the sense of urgency, compulsion. "Not that Jesus resisted but that His pure soul abhorred the personal contact with the Evil One."

XII.   Power for service.

(a) II Tim. 1: 7, Power in general, with a possible particular reference to courageousness.

(b) I Peter 1: 12, I Thes. 1: 5; I Cor. 2: 4, Power in preaching.

(c) Acts 1: 8, Power in witnessing, referring here to every needed qualification,— equipment in general.

XIII.   Confidence and assurance in preaching. I Thes. 1: 5 (Meyer and Lange.) This is the preferred interpretation rather than that the hearers receive the Gospel with assurance, as Riddle and others say.

XIV.   Calls, appoints and qualifies for office, Acts 20: 28.

XV.   Love of the brethren. Rom. 15: 30; II Cor. 6: 6; Col. 1: 8, and II Tim. 1: 7. In this last reference Meyer, Olshausen, Bengel, Smeaton and Cumming say the reference is to the Holy

Spirit; however we look at the passage it virtually amounts to this, for such a spirit we could not receive save through the Holy Spirit imparted to us who Himself has these characteristics.

XVI.   Gives consciousness of God's love. Rom. 5: 5; Cumming's idea of the Spirit loving us is certainly beautiful and legitimate; it does not rest so much on exegetical ground as in that it must be really so. The Spirit cannot produce love in us unless He Himself is loving and loves. This is true of all the fruit of the Spirit.

XVII.   A comprehension and appreciation of Christ's love. Eph. 3: 18, 19.

XVIII.   Peace,—peace in general; peace with God, with man, and inner peace; also Rom. 8: 6. Gal. 5: 22, refers to inner peace solely.

XIX.   Holy joy. Acts 13: 52; Rom. 14: 17.

(a)   Eph. 5: 19, A heart of melody.
(b)   I Thes. 1: 6, Joy in affliction.

Jesus rejoiced in the Holy Spirit; so rendered by the best MSS.

XX.   Hope. Rom. 15: 13.

XXI.   Meekness. Gal. 6: 1, and I Cor. 4: 21. Meyer, Hodge and Smeaton read here the Holy Spirit, while Riddle, Ellicott, Alford, Lange, Lightfoot and others, say it is best to read "spirit of meekness," referring to the human spirit, so read the authorized and revised versions, and this is the more probable, although Meyer and Hodge say, —and there is strength in the assertion,—that when spirit is used with an abstract noun in the genitive it always means Holy Spirit, as Spirit of truth, John 15: 26; 16: 13; I John 4: 6, of adoption,

Rom. 8: 15, of faith, II Cor. 4: 13, of wisdom,
Eph. 1: 17; of power, II Tim. 1: 7.

XXII. Comfort. Acts 9: 31,—Meyer, Alford,
Lange, Gloag, Riddle, make the word mean exhortation; Hackett renders it "aid," referring it either
to consolatory exhortation by the disciples inspired
by the Spirit, or the people being moved by the
Spirit's inward exhortation; but the idea of comfort
is in the word, and is so used in the New Testament,
John 14: 16, 17, and to be so rendered suits well
the context,—the circumstance of the church; so
also Cumming, page 170.

XXIII. Liberty. II Cor. 3: 17, The liberty
which comes from a change of state and relationship, such as pertains to justification.

XXIV. Thanksgiving for all things. Eph. 5: 20.

XXV. A submissive heart. Eph. 5: 21; Phil.
2: 3.

   (a) Wives submitting to husbands, Eph. 5: 22.
   (b) Husbands loving wives, 5: 25.
   (c) Children obeying fathers, 6: 1.
   (d) Fathers not provoking children, 6: 4.
   (e) Servants obeying masters, 6: 5.
   (f) Masters forbearing toward servants, 6: 9.

XXVI. Aid in trouble. Phil. 1: 19, especially
in Paul's case, comfort and courage.

XXVII. Unity.

   (a) Eph. 2: 22, For the sake of strength.
   (b) Eph. 4: 3, In the church and among in-
        dividuals.

XXVIII. Access to God. Eph. 2: 18, that is,
led up to God by the Spirit.

XXIX.   Aid in prayer.

(a) Jude 20 and Rom. 8: 26. The Holy Spirit discovers to us our poverty and the value of spiritual things, promotes the substance of all true prayer and incites to true faith.

(b) Eph. 6: 18, Personal prayer and intercession; it will not do with Cumming, (Through the Eternal Spirit, page 240), to say that intercession is here the special thing. See also Eph. 2: 18; and if prayer is implied in Gal. 4: 6, and Rom. 8: 26, these passages also belong here.

XXX.   Worship by the Spirit. Phil. 3: 3. He prompts, animates and directs it; singing, praying, and all forms of worship are included, though Paul significantly chose the word used to describe Jewish worship by ritual and ceremony; even in these outward forms the Spirit was to be recognized.

XXXI.   Communion. II Cor. 13: 14. Though the thought of fellowship in the sense of communion with the Holy Spirit is not the primary one, such thought is necessarily involved in the word. See preceding chapter. Here also belongs, Phil. 2: 1.

XXXII.   Discipline. II Tim. 1: 7. The word implies more than self-control, having an active signification, and describes a quality calculated to bring others to soberness and soundness of mind.

XXXIII.   Faithfulness in duty. II Tim. 1: 14, Guarding one's trust; probably in Timothy's case the Gospel and his ministry.

XXXIV.   II Cor. 6: 6. Just what relation "by (en) the Holy Spirit" bears to the rest of the discourse is uncertain; not in so many words is it said

those graces are fruits of the Spirit, but if Paul
here introduces the Spirit as the source of them
then we have a list of fruits as follows:

(a) Patience.
(b) Pureness,—both moral sincerity and chastity.
(c) Knowledge,—evangelical, that is, of God's
     moral will.
(d) Kindness.
(e) Love of the brethren.

XXXV.   Patient waiting for future redemption.
Gal. 5: 5.

XXXVI.   First fruits of the Spirit. Rom. 8: 23.
Olshausen, DeWette and Meyer refer this to the
early Christians receiving the Spirit in contrast to
all Christians receiving Him now and later, that is,
a partitive genitive being used. Riddle says what
we now possess is but first fruits of what we shall
receive in glory; also partitive genitive. Hodge,
Godet and Lange say the Holy Spirit is the "first
fruits," as in Eph. 1: 14, an earnest of what we shall
be: appositional genitive. The second and third
views are exactly alike in consequence, and as the
word "first fruits" is always used with a partitive
genitive we prefer Riddle's view.

XXXVII.   Redemption of the body at the resurrection. Rom. 8: 11. Jesus so raised, Rom. 8: 11;
also I Peter 3: 18, according to Smeaton, Cumming
and the authorized version, but strongly opposed
by Meyer, Riddle and the revised version.

XXXVIII.   Eternal life in glory. Gal. 6: 8.
Meyer would put Rom. 8: 6, here also, but the
reference is hardly to be so limited, referring the
rather to eternal life,—spiritual here, and consequently
hereafter of course.

XXXIX. Inspiration. II Peter 1: 21, The word is "borne on"—the figure of a ship before the wind.

XL. Christ was justified in the Spirit. I Tim. 3: 16.

- (a) In His miracles. (b) In His spotless life.
- (c) In His resurrection.
- (a) Our justification by the Spirit is seen by Hodge, Lange, and Alford in I Cor. 6: 11, but, as noted above, it has seemed preferable to take the word as Meyer does in its sense of sanctification.
- (b) Rom. 14: 17, The above three authorities take righteousness in this verse also in the sense of justification, though neither of them connect it with "in the Spirit"; this last phrase, however, is better connected with all three of the preceding words and "righteousness" taken in the sense of holiness (Meyer and Godet).

XLI. I Cor. 12: 8, 9, 10, These we are inclined to believe are apostolic.

9

THE BAPTISM OF THE HOLY SPIRIT

THE word baptism in connection with the name of
the Holy Spirit is mentioned seven times in the
New Testament, Matt. 3: 11; Mark 1: 8; Luke 3:
16; John 1: 33, each referring to John's testimony
that the Coming One was to baptize with the Holy
Spirit. In Acts 1: 5, the risen Christ promises it;
in Acts 11: 16, Peter quotes the promise as having
been fulfilled in the case of Cornelius, and in I Cor.
12: 13, we are said to be baptized "en" one spirit
into one body. The preposition following the word
baptize is in each case "en" save one, Mark 1: 8,
where it is omitted, the Holy Spirit, however, in
each instance being in the same grammatical form
—dative, variously translated in, with and by.
With Pentecost came the fulfilment of the promised
baptism. These disciples we know were:

1. Baptized with the Holy Spirit, Acts 1: 5.
2. Endued, clothed upon,—Revised Version,—
   with power from on high, Lu. 24: 49.
3. Filled with the Spirit, Acts 2: 4, "Pletho,"
   same word used in John 19: 29.

In their case at least the words, "baptism,"
"enduement," "filling," referred to one and the
same experience. This experience was accompanied
by certain miraculous manifestations, "sound as of

rushing wind," "tongues of fire," and followed by certain miraculous results, such as "speaking in foreign tongues."

This was fitting, first, as the inaugural of a new dispensation; second, because the disciples were in need of the miraculous—how very much one can easily imagine. We are to bear in mind that the miracles were the *accompaniments* and the *results* of the baptism.

The chief purpose of this baptism was qualification for the best possible service.

The results in case of the disciples were:

(a) Miraculous powers, Acts 2: 4.
(b) Witnessing. (1) With boldness, Acts 2: 4.
  (2) With power, Acts 1: 8; 2: 41; and no doubt to each of them was given other gifts not then recorded, Acts 19: 6; I Cor. 12: 1, 12.

Was this baptism their regeneration or were the disciples regenerated men before Pentecost? Rev. G. Campbell Morgan takes the former view ("The Spirit of God," pages 132 and 174). Even were his conception true it would by no means be a necessary deduction therefrom that regeneration was the thing of chief import at Pentecost. We are forced to feel that Dr. Morgan has emphasized the wrong thing. Certainly a believer after Pentecost would be a broader visioned and deeper experienced individual than one before. He would in some respects be a new man. Christ means immeasurably more to the Christian of to-day than He could possibly mean to the disciples in the period of his incarnation. Regeneration is by an almost unanimous opinion considered to be an act resulting in the instantaneous change from spiritual death to spiritual life. Its metaphysical nature must forever remain a mystery, and before thinking of the disciples as unregenerated one must rather thoroughly understand the nature of this mysterious and divinely inwrought work and rather thoroughly appreciate the scope of the change resulting therefrom. Says Andrew Murray, page 323, "To the disciples the Baptism of the Spirit was very distinctly not His first bestowal for regeneration but the definite communication of the Presence in power of their glorified Lord."

Certainly the disciples had received the Holy Spirit before Pentecost; if not, how interpret John 20: 22? "He breathed on them and said receive ye the Holy Spirit." This Dr. Morgan calls a "prophetic breathing," a "typical act," page 108, and Dr. Cumming also concurs in this, saying the disciples here received nothing; but, first, the aorist imperative of the verb "receive" argues against such a conception; second, the thought embodied in the verb "send" argues against it: third, the act of breathing is against it. (Same verb used in Gen. 2: 7.) Fourth, if nothing were received it would be only a repetition of the Saviour's promise in his farewell discourse.

Some argue the omission of the article before the Holy Spirit, making it refer not to the personal Holy Spirit, but to His influence only, but such omission is of little or no import. Entirely too much stress has been laid upon every slight variation of expression. Seemingly unmindful that under the inspiration of the Holy Spirit the writer was not a machine, there have always been critics who could see the hand of several writers in one treatise or

build an inverted pyramid of manuscript in defense
of a theory resting upon the slightest grammatical
deviation from the author's established style. (For
a most excellent exposition on the use of the article
in the New Testament see Cumming, "Through
the Eternal Spirit," page 281.) Scofield says, "They
first received the Holy Spirit here." ("Plain Papers
on the Doctrine of the Holy Spirit," page 35.)
With Bengel, Calvin, Olshausen, Stier, Alford,
Godet, Meyer and others we see in the passage
in question an impartation of the Holy Spirit, not
so full and complete as at Pentecost, but quantitative
at least, an impartation already to regenerate men
or at least an impartation which effected that regeneration. (See Swete in Hastings' "Dictionary of the
Bible"—Article on "Holy Spirit." In Kuyper's
recent studied work on the Holy Spirit, he gives
a threefold relation of the Holy Spirit to the disciples.

(1) Regeneration and subsequent illumination,
Matt. 16: 17.

(2) Reception as official gift qualifying them for
apostolic office, John 20: 22.

(3) Pentecost.

Torrey—"Baptism of the Holy Spirit," page 6,
refers to John 13: 10; 15: 3, "ye are clean," as
witnessing the disciples' regeneration. With him is
nearly all critical authority. Cumming, page 98,
speaking of the disciples at Pentecost, says, "They
were new men, not in the sense of being born
again, for assuredly they had all known that change
before."

We repeat, however, that even were this subjective
change first wrought at Pentecost this would in no
way militate against the fact that *the distinctive
feature of that occasion was not regeneration, but*

enduement for service. We must confess that the startling thing about Dr. Morgan's book, "The Spirit of God," is the bold maneuver in exegesis by which he undertakes to substantiate the claim he has made. We have looked for his authority and have failed to find it. It is always inspiring to see a man who dares to differ from centuries of authority. However, in coming to safe views of Scriptural truths, we must have respect to what others have thought before us. In the attempt to establish a theory all men are susceptible to bias and the comforting thing to the student in the critical exegesis of Scripture upon the subject is that he is coming in contact with the opinions of scholars who for the most part, and certainly so far as this subject is concerned, were seeking to establish no theory, but searching from an independent viewpoint what things the Scripture really said.

Dr. Morgan, in support of his view, has surprisingly quoted a great number of baptismal passages in the New Testament as referring to the baptism of the Holy Spirit. He quotes Rom. 6: 3, 4. We have not found it possible to agree with such an interpretation of this passage. It is not the purpose of these pages to be controversial nor will their limits admit of extended argument, but in consideration of what has just been said of exegetical opinion it is desired simply to say that the reverend scholar's position is taken in the face of overwhelming authority if such a thing there can be. This passage in Romans is taken to mean "water baptism," by Bengel, Calvin, Tholuck, Ruckert, Lightfoot, Lange, Meyer, Barnes, Stuart, Shedd, Schaff, Conybeare and Howson, Webster and Wilkinson, Hodge, Elli-Moule in his recent volume, Marvin

R. Vincent in his Word Studies (just published) *and all others consulted.*

"Baptism into" means baptism *in reference to* and the phrase in no way teaches baptismal regeneration. As clear-viewed, Calvin said, "We ought in baptism to recognize a spiritual law; we ought in it to embrace a witness to the remission of sins and a pledge of our renewal, and yet so to leave both to Christ and the Holy Spirit the honor that is theirs as that no part of the salvation be transferred to the sign."

Gal. 3: 27; I Peter 3: 21, and Eph. 4: 5, are other passages quoted in face of the same array of authority. In Matt. 28: 19, amongst the last words of Jesus was the command to the disciples that they should "teach all nations, baptizing them in the name of the Father and of the Son and of the Holy Spirit." In Mark 16: 16, among His last words are, "He that believeth and is baptized shall be saved." This last Dr. Morgan calls the Baptism of the Holy Spirit (Spirit of God,—page 118); the passage in Matthew cannot of course be so construed and what worthy reasons exist for considering the passage in Mark any different does not appear.

Scofield says (Plain Papers on the Doctrine of the Spirit—page 41) that from Pentecost to the case of Cornelius,—Acts 10, opening the door to the Gentiles,—two peculiarities mark the impartation of the Spirit to believers, one of which was that "commonly an interval of time elapsed between the receiving of Christ by faith and the baptism of the Spirit." Beginning with chapter ten he says the baptism came at the moment of regeneration. This is true in the case of Cornelius (Acts 10: 44 and 11: 15), but was it the same kind of Baptism that came at Pentecost? If so, then although it came practically simultaneous with regeneration, it must have been something different from regeneration and conditioned by it. That the baptism in chapter ten was the same as that which the disciples and all others since Pentecost had received is evidenced by the miraculous gifts which came with it and by Peter's account of it in the next chapter.

What has thus far been said has been offered in the defence of the view that the disciples at Pentecost were not necessarily unregenerate, and more particularly that the Baptism of the Holy Spirit they and all others (recorded) received, was *not* identical with regeneration.

We now come to what has been our common error—the old failure of definition; Scofield, (Plain Papers on the Doctrine of the Spirit,—page 42) beginning with Acts 10 as a starting point, (where, as we have seen, mention is made of a Baptism of the Holy Spirit identical with that of Pentecost,) seeks to establish the fact that all believers are now and have been from that time, Acts 10, regenerated and baptized by the Spirit at one and the same time, and adduces in defence of such position the exceeding difficult passage in I Cor. 12: 13. This passage Morgan, (Spirit of God,—page 174), also quotes as proof that regeneration and Spirit Baptism are identical. If I Cor. 12: 13, refers to the Baptism of the Holy Spirit, it *is* identical with regeneration, but do we not at once see that as such it is an altogether different kind of baptism from that of the Holy Spirit in Acts 10, or any time previous; in other words, if this baptism in I Cor. 12: 13, is that of the Spirit, it is different from every other experience in the Word of God bearing that name.

Granting now for the moment that the word "baptism" in I Cor. 12: 13, has no reference to water, but refers solely to the regenerative work of the Spirit, we would have, in view of the above discussion and the present concession:

(1) A Baptism of the Holy Spirit beginning at Pentecost (and ending, so far as the name is concerned, at Acts 10), differing from regeneration, and either subsequent to regeneration or practically simultaneous with it (Acts 10) though conditioned by it. This baptism was a special enduement or filling of the Holy Spirit for service.

(2) A Baptism of the Holy Spirit simultaneous and *identical* with regeneration, a spiritual baptismal regeneration, which belongs not only to every believer since Acts 10, but has occurred in the case of every individual ever regenerated. Not every treatise has made this distinction clear. It is in fact the distinction noted by Cumming, page 117, between Christ baptizing men with the Holy Spirit and the Holy Spirit baptizing men into Christ. The first might properly be called the Baptism *with* the Holy Spirit, and the second the Baptism *of* the Holy Spirit. The first is Christ's baptism; the second is the Spirit's baptism. The Baptism *of* the Holy Spirit is therefore, properly speaking, the same as regeneration, whatever may be the interpretation given to I Cor. 12: 13, and even though there be in the Scripture no specific mention of it in the exact phraseology we are using. In speaking, therefore, of the post-regenerative experience *under discussion* the reader will note that through the remainder of these remarks the expression, "Baptism *with* the

Holy Spirit" is used. Now concerning I Cor. 12: 13, "For with one Spirit we were all baptized into one body." The Revised Version reads, "in one Spirit,"—but as it is the same preposition as is used in every other case, we see no reason for reading other than "with" (as expressive of the agent) in this instance, especially if it means baptism in the sense above granted.

Does it refer to water baptism or to the regenerative impartation of the Holy Spirit? The question is a difficult one, and no man can decide it and as the translator of Kling has said, "It will continue to be determined in accordance with the feeling and original preferences of different individuals." Authority, which preponderates in favor of the first, is divided so far as we have discovered as follows: For water baptism, Bengel, Meyer, Alford, DeWette, Kling, Ruckert, Luther, Beza, Calvin, Henry, Scott, Cumming, Vincent. For the regenerative baptism of the Holy Ghost apart altogether from water baptism, Hodge, Chapman, Scofield, Morgan, MacNeil.

In Gal. 3: 27, and Eph. 4: 5, where the reference as we have taken it is to water baptism, Paul says we are "baptized into Christ," and here he says, "we are baptized into Christ 'en' the Holy Spirit," and as it is not plain that he anywhere else speaks of the regenerative act as a baptism it would seem the part of consistent exegesis to see a reference to water baptism here.

This baptism is then either "in" the Holy Spirit as the element into which the baptized have been transferred and in which they are ever after expected to live (the E. R. V. rendering seems to favor this as in every other instance where the same preposition is used "with" is given as the preferred meaning);

or it is "with" or "by" the Holy Spirit in the
sense that the Holy Spirit is the agent of the faith
which is the necessary accompaniment of every
baptism into Christ. This is the explanation of
Cumming (Through the Eternal Spirit, page 117).

Impossible to come to an unquestioned decision,
we must content ourselves with a preference. That
preference is for the explanation of Cumming. In
the word "baptism" therefore, in this verse is to
be found an immediate reference to water baptism.
This brings the conclusion that as a regenerative
act the baptism of the Holy Spirit is nowhere mentioned in the Scripture. Hodge says, "any communication of the Spirit may be called a baptism
whether in his regenerating, sanctifying or inspiring
influences." This is true, but his regenerating
influence is not so called in Scripture and what we
must in our now current discussions avoid is a
confusion of terms.

The Holy Spirit does baptize us into Christ whether
so mentioned in Scripture or not, but this experience
in reality is prior to that of which Paul speaks in
I Cor. 12: 13, inasmuch as when a man comes to
the baptismal place he is supposed to be already
a regenerated individual; he is then on the ground
of his faith, previously produced by the Holy Spirit,
baptized into, that is, in respect to Christ. The
other view which must also be worthily considered
maintains that Paul here has no reference to water
and speaks solely of the regenerative baptism by
the Holy Spirit into Christ, which of course is
experienced by everyone who believes.

Our discussion has so far thus resolved itself:
1. Every believer has had one Baptism *of* the Spirit
(regenerative) whether the particular phraseology be

so used in Scripture or not. 2. If I Cor. 12: 13, refers immediately to regeneration there is at least *one* express mention of this baptism in the Word. 3. To the apostles and early Christians was granted a Baptism *with* the Spirit (post-regenerative) filling them with power and preparing them for every emergency in Christian experience.

Now comes the other question, Is there such a thing as Christ baptizing men *with* the Holy Spirit to-day? May we be baptized as were the apostles? As far as the phrasing of that experience is concerned, it nowhere in Scripture says we may; but it is the writer's opinion based upon his own experience that many an anxious one has been led into confusion about this most important matter by expressions of different writers seemingly antagonistic because of an indiscriminating use of terms or a lack of explanation as to the exact meaning involved. For example, note the following:

(1) "The believer may ask and expect what may be termed a Baptism of the Spirit," Murray,—Spirit of Christ,—page 323.

(2) "The Baptism is not like the filling presented to us as a blessing for which the Christian is to seek," Moule,—Veni Creator,—page 222.

(3) "Neither is there any gift He is more willing to bestow upon believers than this Divine Baptism"; Mahan,—Baptism of the Holy Ghost,—pages 48 and 49.

(4) "It is not right that Christian people should profess to be waiting for the Baptism of the Spirit"; Morgan,—The Spirit of God,—page 176.

(5) "The Baptism of the Spirit is the beginning of the full life of Christian experience"; Cumming, —Through the Eternal Spirit,—page 119.

(6) "It is unscriptural for the Christian to be talking about the Baptism of the Holy Ghost"; Chapman,—Received ye the Holy Ghost,—page 75.

(7) "It surely cannot be unscriptural for a believer to pray, Lord Jesus baptize me with the Holy Spirit"; MacNeil,—Spirit-filled Life,—page 38.

(8) "It does not follow that every believer has received this Baptism of the Spirit"; Gordon,— The Ministry of the Spirit,—page 75. He goes on to show they may.

(9) "And she (a Christian woman) received the Baptism of the Holy Ghost inside of ten minutes"; Torrey,—Baptism with the Holy Ghost,—page 19.

The experience which we are discussing is of vital importance to every believer, and anxious to know that he may have a thoughtful appreciation of the thing he is told to seek, is it any wonder he finds himself somewhat bewildered in the presence of so many statements, some actually conflicting, others apparently so, though a different experience is being described by the same name. Is there a "Baptism with the Holy Spirit" for the believer to-day? We have already said that in this particular phraseology, Scripture does not say there is; bu may we have the experience belonging to it? Paul said in Eph. 5: 18, "Be filled with the Spirit." Before attempting an answer to the above question let us endeavor to see something of what Paul meant by the experience to which he exhorts us in the words, "Be filled with the Spirit."

10

THE FILLING OF THE HOLY SPIRIT

In the chapter on the advent of the Spirit were noted three distinct periods of the Spirit's presence and operation. In each of these men were filled with the Spirit.

I. In the Old Testament, Bezaleel, Ex. 28: 3; 31: 3; 35: 31. See also Deut. 34: 9. Eight times in the Old Testament the Spirit is said to be in men, twenty-seven times upon men, and three times to be clothed with men. These different expressions make no difference in the resulting experience.

II. From the Incarnation to Pentecost, John the Baptist, Luke 1: 15; Elizabeth, Luke 1: 41; Zacharias, Luke 1: 67. In all these instances the same Greek word, "pletho" (to fill) or its Hebrew equivalent, "male," as in the case of Bezaleel, is used, and in each case, according to the Spirit's economy prior to Pentecost, was the equipment of a special individual to do a special work.

III. Pentecost and after. At Pentecost the disciples were baptized, Acts 1: 5, endued with power, Luke 24: 49; and filled, Acts 2: 4; all in one and the same experience. This filling was accompanied by miraculous signs and followed by miraculous effects, but there was nothing miraculous about the filling itself. The writer means in this sense—for instance, supposing Paul's regeneration to have occurred on his way to Damascus, there was nothing more miraculous about it than about yours or mine,—the miracle (the blazing light, etc.), was the accompaniment. These spiritual processes or acts are always in a sense miraculous, but the actual filling and the actual regenerating were according to the regular method of operation, and if there is such an experience for the believer to-day, it will be the same kind of filling, given by the same method which the disciples received by whatever name it may be called.

In Acts 4: 8 Peter was filled again, and again with all the disciples, in 4: 31. Paul was filled in Acts 9: 17, and once more in 13: 9. We now call attention to the fact that Stephen in Acts 6: 5, and 7: 55, and Barnabas in Acts 11: 24, are said to be men "full of the Holy Spirit," the adjective ($\pi\lambda\eta\rho\eta s$) being used, whereas in the above-noted fillings, when used as a qualifying clause, the past participle ($\pi\lambda\eta\theta\epsilon\iota s$) is employed as designative of something definitely done. Some have accordingly found a distinction here which to a certain extent is a worthy one, though it sounds very strange to speak of a difference between being "full of the Spirit" and being "filled with the Spirit." The first refers more properly to the habitual fullness of the Spirit as a somewhat permanent state of the soul; the second to occasional experiences for special purposes.

We remark, (1) It is not difficult to conceive of the distinction. We speak of a man well known for his godliness and spiritual power as being full of the Holy Spirit, without implying that he is filled to the utmost reach of his capacity for fulness as may be needful for him on some particular occasion. Peter was filled more than once and certainly after Pentecost he was, even as Barnabas and Stephen, a man "full of the Holy Spirit," though this particular expression is nowhere used of him in Scripture. And may we not think of Barnabas and Stephen, men *full of the Spirit*, Acts 11: 24; 6: 5; 7: 55, being on some special occasion *filled with the Spirit* for some special purpose. Says F. B. Meyer,—"A Castaway," page 100, "You may be a man full of the Holy Ghost in your family, but before entering your pulpit, be sure that you are especially equipped by a new reception of the Holy Ghost." The filling then with this distinction in mind would correspond more nearly to what most people understand as the anointing—the special equipment for a special purpose. Such was Acts 2: 4; 4: 8; 13: 9, etc., while the fulness would find its reference to the more ordinary condition of every godly character—to what Cumming calls, page 230, "the habit of the soul."

(2) The distinction, if accepted, we are inclined to think is one altogether of degree; the occasional filling being simply an increased supply of the same power already in possession such as the exigency of the occasion demands. It presupposes the need with which it comes and with which it departs; it presupposes, of course, the fulness as the more habitual possession and is received upon exactly the same conditions with it.

What then was this experience which came to the disciples when in fulfillment of the promise that they should "be baptized with the Holy Spirit not many days hence" it is said in Scripture, Acts 2: 4, "They were all filled with the Holy Spirit?"

What happened to the disciples when thus filled? It is not the name of an experience we are trying to establish, but its nature we would so far as possible understand. Have we not gone to unwarranted lengths in seeking to establish a difference in import in the meaning of "in," "with" and "by," and various other modes of expression by which in Scripture it is evidently desired to convey the same thought? In the case of the household of Cornelius Peter describes the one experience by "poured out," "fell upon," "received," "baptized," and "gave," and then said it was like Pentecost which therefore was also an "enduement" and a "filling."

But when the disciples were filled at Pentecost what we do know is that the Holy Spirit as a divine personal Presence, so wrought upon or exercised Himself within them or so influenced them that the inner subjective change resultant therefrom fitted them for service and of course for holy living also, although note this last is never mentioned as as result of the filling received by the Apostles. The Holy Spirit then for the first time manifested Himself in fulness in the men of God and filled them for the particular service of the hour; had it been some great spiritual conflict through which they were to pass the filling which they received would have been appropriate and adequate to that; had it been to endure martyrdom or suffer otherwise the filling would have been given for that, for although the occasion made equipment for service the prominent need it is not our thought that the filling of the Spirit is to be thus limited.

Now when Paul tells us in Eph. 5: 18, to "Be filled with the Spirit," it is doubtless with more immediate reference to that habitual fulness which

ought to characterize the life of every believer.
What he meant was "live the Spirit-filled life."
But if the Spirit-filled life is held before us as a
possible attainment, certainly the special filling needful at crisal moments in Christian experience,
which, after all, though the above distinction be
thoroughly appreciated, is the more ordinary fulness
carried up to its highest manifestation, will not be
denied us if in the time of need we put ourselves
in a condition to receive it, and what other could
the Pentecostal experience and the special fillings
that came to the Disciples be than a *high degree*
of the same power which is necessarily associated
with that fulness of the Spirit (Eph. 5: 18) which
is the normal or healthy condition of soul and
which ought to characterize the life of every believer.

It is an experience wrought upon our very inmost
self. Its metaphysical nature is beyond finite comprehension. It is God Himself in the presence and
Person of His Holy Spirit entering into the throne
room of a believer's being, ruling there with power
for the perfection of life and commanding for the
advancement of His kingdom the now divinely
energized faculties of a God-possessed and God-
empowered soul.

In view of this it certainly will not be missing
the truth if it is said with Cumming ("Through the
Eternal Spirit," page 114), that for the Christian
of to-day "in addition to the gift of the Spirit received
at conversion there is another blessing corresponding
in its sign and effects to the blessing received by
the apostles at Pentecost," or with Boardman, "(In
the Power of the Spirit," page 2), that "All of every
age who have shown by their fruits that they have
had the apostolic enduement of spiritual power,

came into it by an experimental reception of the Holy Spirit not essentially different from that of the apostles and evangelists."

If this filling received by the disciple to-day is not essentially different from the experience accorded to the early disciples by what name shall we call it? As learned Dr. Hodge has reminded us, any impartation of the Holy Spirit is a baptism, and certainly, apart from biblical phraseology, a filling with the Spirit may be called a baptism with the Spirit. Again since a not essentially different experience in the case of the disciples *is* called a baptism would it not seem to be of Scriptural warrant, to call this filling also a baptism? But since Scripture does not use the term baptism, in the sense in which we are now speaking, when referring to this experience, in that portion of God's Word especially designed for the saints of this day —the Epistles—but does exhort the Christian to be filled with the Spirit, many have argued, especially since there is a question in the minds of some as to the similarity of these experiences, that it would be best to adhere in present-day terminology to the word "filling"; but if the use of such a term is calculated to magnify a difference which does not exist, such a distinction in choice of words had better be abandoned. What is there, therefore, but to conclude with Andrew Murray,—"Spirit of Christ," page 23,—that the believer may come into an experience of "what may be termed a baptism with the Holy Spirit."

Possible objections to the above conclusion:

1. It has been objected that the word baptism is not used in this connection with reference to believers in any of the Epistles. It is true the New Testament

writers were very choice in their use of words, but this very fact cripples the objection, since Luke has made use of so many different expressions to describe the one experience under consideration. Since also the term "filling" is used interchangeably with "baptism" in the Acts, and the mere fact that this was an experience for the disciples is no reason in itself why it may not be ours, and since, after all, the point of discussion is an *experience* and not a *word*, the above objection is of insufficient force for any invalidation of the position we have assumed.

2. It has been objected that a feature of the early baptism with the Spirit was the miraculous. The miraculous was not, however, essential to the thing itself; it was the accompaniment and a method of manifestation according to the economy of that day. If it is the miraculous that determines the experience, then it is heartily conceded that there is no baptism for the believer today, but a filling differing from the baptism in this particular. But the miraculous does not belong to the nature of the filling, and with no difference in the experience that comes to a Spirit-filled man today God could, if He chose, use him in setting the miraculous before the world, the subjective condition of the man being in no wise different from that which characterized the saints of earlier days.

That the filling is not accompanied by miraculous manifestations today is true; that it is not followed by them is also true. Some of our recognized teachers upon this subject have affirmed the opposite concerning the miraculous results of this experience; they claim to have witnessed such results. Possibly they have failed in close discrimination between the miraculous and the working of natural law.

Neither their conviction nor their veracity is called in question, but the writer finds himself simply unable to believe it; he does believe the prayer of faith shall save the sick; he does believe in the physiological effect of faith and in the power of mental states over physical conditions; but when a man, Spirit-filled though he be, goes with me to the side of a mutilated, flesh-corroded leper or any person suffering with an organic ailment, and lifts him at once into the vigor of health, he will find another ardent believer of the genuinely miraculous result of the experience under consideration.

Bishop Taylor, according to Rev. Mr. Godbey, tells of a young lady, who, in three months, preached fluently to a nation of whose language she had been utterly ignorant. This Mr. Godbey calls the "Gift of Tongues." A Spirit-filled person can learn a great deal in three months by hard work, but the disciples spoke not only in one but in many tongues in less time than that. That such miraculous power did attend the gift of the Holy Spirit in the early church, Paul's letters render plain, I Cor. 12: 1–12. Whether the church has lost them through her unfaithfulness or whether, which is more probable, as Dr. Meyer suggests, "special gifts being given for special purposes they are now withdrawn," is a question without a place in the purpose of this discussion.

3. It has been objected that the filling enjoined by Paul in Eph. 5: 18, had for its chief aim the development of character, while that of apostolic times was always connected with service. But in recording the growth of the church service would naturally be the point of emphasis though certainly a holy character must have been presupposed; while

Paul in his thought for the Ephesian Christians would naturally emphasize that which is the foundation of all service. Luke was writing *of* the church; Paul was writing *to* the church; the purpose and consequent nature of the writings satisfactorily account for this difference. If this be kept in mind, together with the explanation as given in the beginning of this chapter, the above objection in no sense invalidates the argument set forth in these pages.

4. It has been objected that the conditions of these experiences are different; to be filled with the Spirit, as understood today, calls for the fullest surrender and the most thorough consecration, while in apostolic times it was granted to those who were evidently the most ordinary Christians. In answer to this it may be said:

(a) There is no clear evidence that the three thousand at Pentecost were thus filled.

(b) It has been thought that at such an initial time, to lend the kingdom all possible advance it may have seemed wise to the Head of the Church to bestow this gift on less stringent conditions.

(c) The better answer, however, is that the objection involves an unwarranted assumption; there is no evidence that those filled were other than they who were of the required character for this experience.

In view of the first three objections, should any consider them formidable, there is no baptism with the Spirit for the believer today, but as already explained, the *name* and the *miracle*, as the point of emphasis, have no part in the nature of the act or process,—for it is both,—and if this last is not essentially different in either case, then the experience itself is virtually the same. If the Spirit's operations are essentially the same both in the baptism and the filling the name is of small importance; it is not a question of nomenclature, but of a spiritual act and process which remain in nature unchanged by whatever term it may be designated.

We observe then:

(1) There are many fillings. Two instances of Paul's filling have been noted, Acts 9: 17, and 13: 9; the disciples were filled, Acts 2: 4, and again, 4: 31; and Peter, a third time, Acts 4: 8, each being an experience similar to Pentecost, says Kuyper, only weaker. These repeated fillings were all in view of service to be performed. That it was because these men had "passed into a realm of fear and trembling," Morgan, (Spirit of God, page 189), that such filling must again be renewed we cannot with certainty affirm; it is not so difficult to conceive of being always "full of the Spirit" as the normal condition or habit of the soul, but that any one, even Peter or Paul, should, despite the limitations of the human nature, remain continually in the overflowing condition, at the utmost height of spiritual power and attainment, should at every minute of life be filled with the Spirit to the measure which at some particular crisis is necessary to the highest glory of God is hardly possible to conceive. Such filling is, however, for us at whatever moment we need it and are ready to receive it.

The Filling of the Spirit and what some have chosen to call and we have conceded may be called, the Baptism with the Spirit, being therefore one and the same kind of experience we fail to see the ground for saying, as does Cumming, (Through the Eternal

Spirit, page 119), that there is but one baptism and many fillings, and that "the baptism is something not to be repeated in the experience of the man who receives it." MacNeil, (Spirit-filled Life, page 37), says, "The filling may be and ought to be repeated over and over and over again; the baptism need be but once"; and again he says, page 39, "He must not continue praying for the baptism, for that cannot be repeated; whereas, he may ask and obtain a fresh filling, a refilling with the Holy Spirit every day of his life." Erdman, Morgan, Chapman, Carson, all say, "one baptism and many fillings"; so also do Cumming and MacNeil.

This is the oft-quoted formula of Dr. Erdman; *but notice the above-mentioned writers do not all mean alike ;* the first group refer the baptism to regeneration, I Cor. 12: 13, for which there is reason, as already seen, and if admitted, the formula is true; Cumming and MacNeil, however, use the same formula and refer the baptism to the special experience after regeneration, in which case the distinction is not a worthy one.

They say the baptism is the beginning of the full experience, and there can be only one beginning and therefore one baptism; but this makes no distinction in the experience. Certainly there can be but one first, so also is there but one second, and along the line of Dr. Cumming's argument, with which we have in the main agreed, we find no room for saying the baptism of the Spirit can never be repeated.

These baptisms, these fillings, by whatever name they are called are all alike save in measure, and the last one may be greater than the first. We have all heard of the Second Blessing, counting regeneration the first, but someone has wisely said, "I believe not only in a second but in a forty-second blessing."

(2) This experience, this filling or baptism, is subsequent to regeneration. It may be received for the first time on the same occasion with our regeneration, but never in the same moment. Both logically and chronologically it is a subsequent operation of the Spirit. "The reason," says William Kelly in his lectures on the "New Testament Doctrine of the Holy Spirit," page 161, "is quite simple, for it is grounded on the fact that we are sons by faith in Christ, believers resting on redemption in Him."

Between the regeneration of the disciples and their filling some time elapsed, Acts 2: 4; it was so in the case of Paul, Acts 9: 17. If Paul's conversion occurred in the house of Judas, as Morgan would have us believe, and the filling likewise, still the latter would be subsequent to and dependent upon the former; if he were born of the Spirit on the way to Damascus, as is probable, and which Morgan does not vehemently oppose, then how, according to Morgan, could the filling be simultaneous with the regeneration? (The Spirit of God, page 187.)

The same thing was true in the case of the Samaritan Christians, Acts 8: 12–17. They believed and were baptized in the name of Jesus under the preaching of a Spirit-filled man like Philip, and yet Dr. Morgan says none of them were converted or regenerated, reasoning that Simon Magus also believed, but was not truly regenerated; but his case proves nothing as to the real condition of the others; the trouble with Simon Magus was his "heart was not right," and Peter told him so, but this argues nothing as to the heart condition of the others. The gospel Philip preached was certainly as pure as that which fell from the lips of Peter, and we can see no legitimate ground for not calling these people

Christians, and yet they were given the blessing of which we speak as a later experience.

The same thing is true of the believers in Acts 19: 1-6. Scofield, page 47, and Morgan, page 180, says, "These people were not Christians."

Most authorities hold differently. What we know is that they were disciples of John the Baptist, and in a certain sense it may be said they were not Christians. In which case neither were the disciples Christians before Pentecost, which position we have seen to be untenable. It is best to see in these people, whom Luke calls "disciples" and "believers," certain ones whose spiritual status warranted Paul holding before them the experience under consideration, to which as yet they were strangers and which, as we have seen, comes subsequent to regeneration.

In the case of Cornelius, however, Acts 10: 45-46 and 11: 15, the regeneration and baptism were on the same occasion, practically simultaneous, although even here the logical order, as well as the chronological by accurate distinction must have been first regeneration and then baptism, as was also the case of the Ephesian disciples, Acts 19: 1-6, even though we think of their conversion in connection with the experience brought to them by Paul; for they, first believing what Paul said, were baptized in the name of Jesus, presupposing regeneration of course, and in this act a reception of the Spirit, Rom. 8:9; and then Paul laid his hands upon them, all of which took a few moments at least, and then they received the Holy Spirit in the sense of this discussion.

At the self-same time of a man's conversion he may be given a special filling or baptism to meet some particular demand of the hour, but into the Spirit-filled condition in the sense of the more ordinary fullness (Eph. 5: 18) he not only may enter at conversion, but God expects of him that he shall do so; these both, however, rest upon the fact that he is already born of the Spirit.

(3) Is this condition the normal (healthy) and a possible continuous one? This is not a hard question. In the immediate sense of Eph. 5: 18 (the more ordinary fullness) the answer is, Yes. In the sense of the special filling for a special purpose the answer is, No. Cumming (Through the Eternal Spirit,— page 115), after likening this experience to the filling of the disciples, says, "It is only from want of faith that subsequent outpourings of the Holy Spirit become needful." But if the filling has respect to equipment for some particular purpose, certainly a special outpouring or filling for the particular thing at hand is the original purpose of God. We can understand how the "fullness of the Spirit" as a habit of the soul is the normal and more continuous condition, as with Barnabas and Stephen, and believe we know some today of whom it may be said they are "full of the Holy Spirit," but between this and the more specific filling a difference of degree has already been noted. Says Morgan, page 186, "When a man is born of the Spirit he is baptized with the Spirit and is filled with the Spirit." That when a man is born of the Spirit he has the Spirit is true, else he is none of His, Rom. 8: 9; that he may then be filled with the Spirit is also true, as we have seen, but that he is then filled with the Spirit either in the sense of the fulness of the Spirit, as a habit of the soul, or in the sense of being filled with the Spirit after the fashion now engaging our attention, we can find no warrant either in Scripture or in the possible conception of our own mind.

(4) What is this filling of the Spirit? It is nothing less than the very presence of God Himself working His unhindered will in the human soul, in which is experienced His power of mastery over the sin principle and whatever of the divine energy is necessary for the highest results in service or suffering. Power, energy, force are to be appreciated not defined.

There is power in fire; watch its unconquerable march over a proud city whose mighty buildings of brick and stone and iron are melted at its touch.

There is power in wind, driving the mighty ship across the seas, tearing deep-rooted forests from the earth, hurling huge buildings through space and sweeping whole cities into splintered ruin.

There is power in water,—the power of a flood, who can estimate it?

Yet, if these could speak, they could not tell you what power is; but these are in Scripture made emblems of the Holy Spirit; the supernatural power of the Spirit is symbolized but only symbolized in the mighty dynamics of these natural elements. Undefinable as their energy is, much less can the Divine potency be explained.

What is power? "God hath spoken once, yes, twice have I heard this that power belongeth unto God." Nor can it be divorced from God; nor can any man obtain it save as God Himself comes with it, and the "filling of the Holy Spirit" is the very self of God, *already indwelling the human soul through regeneration*, working out His unhindered will in and through the now divinely controlled faculties in the fullest manifestation of all that man can be and do.

The human will has allowed Him undisputed sway over the entire being so hallowed by His presence, and in turn with every other faculty of the inner man is energized with the very life of God Himself for the accomplishment in character and service of that for which it hath pleased the Almighty to bestow them.

Just here is, after all, the great difference in present-day teaching; much of other discussion springs, as has been noted, from a confusion in nomenclature. The difficult question and the one, after all, to which it is impossible to give an absolute and unqualified answer is this: (1) Is this experience the working of the Spirit already within the believer; or (2) Is it another and special reception of the Spirit Himself; or (3) Is it both? To attempt such an answer as just indicated is for the finite to presume a knowledge sufficient to clarify the most infinite mystery,—the omnipresence of a divine Personality. That it is the second apart from the first we believe to be wholly unscriptural. That it is the first apart from the second is in a sense certainly true; as a divine Personality it is not in part but in His entirety that the Spirit of God dwells in the believer; it is upon this view we are strongly inclined to believe the chief emphasis should rest. We may have more of the Spirit's filling, that is, more of His power, more of His influence, more of the fruit of the Spirit; but to speak of having more of the Spirit Himself, as does Andrew Murray, ("Spirit of Christ," page 321), is to come dangerously near to a species of mysticism hardly consistent with the accredited religious thought of the day.

However, the third of the above views, namely, the first two considered together, is not without argument in its favor. This is the view of Andrew Murray. He says,—"Spirit of Christ," page 320,— "That there is a great deal of prayer in which the presence of the Spirit is forgotten, is ignored, I admit and deplore; and yet it would be falling into the other extreme, if, because God has given and we have received the Spirit, we were no longer to pray for more of Him." F. B. Meyer also says, "Before undertaking any definite work for God be sure you are equipped by a new reception of the Holy Ghost." ("A Castaway," page 100.)

Moule, commenting on Eph. 1: 17, says, "We are not to think of the 'giving' of the Spirit as an isolated deposit of what, once given, is now locally in possession." This is true, as is also Murray's statement that "God has not given His Spirit in the sense of parting with Him."

The Spirit is in heaven as well as in the believer, and He is at the same time in every believer, yet in speaking of a personality as we are, we have found ourselves unable to appreciate Mr. Murray's comparison of the desire for the Spirit's filling to the fingers crying to the heart for more blood, the branch crying to the vine for more sap, and the lungs crying to the air for more breath.

There is in this mode of speaking the danger just referred to and the liability of leaving with the less thoughtful reader the impression of an influence rather than a personality. To define, especially in a theological sense, is always easier than to appreciate the subject of the definition as defined. Nowhere is this more true than in the case before us; how much easier to define the Holy Spirit as a person than to think of the Holy Spirit as such when we are thinking of omnipresence or of soul experiences which we know are from God; and the very fact that this is so, together with the fact that so many, even among those who may have the most correct definition, have accustomed themselves to think thus carelessly about this blessed Presence, should guard us carefully against any mode of expression that might in any way seem to favor such impression.

We have thought long here, but have been left always as at the outset. The subject deals with Infinity, and while many have made statements conformable as they believe to Scripture, it is satisfying to note that not in a single volume is any attempt made to deal with this inscrutable mystery with a view to making it wholly intelligible to the finite mind; we are in the presence of the Infinite, and it becomes us to say, "Speak Lord, for thy servant heareth," and to be satisfied with what He says.

This most precious bestowal we have been accustomed to explain by figurative expressions; indeed, we have been taught in this by the inspired writers themselves. Even baptism and filling are figurative as touching any relation the Holy Spirit can bear to an individual. We speak, as indeed does the Word, of His filling us, clothing us, being poured upon us, etc.; all of which are accommodations to the finite. All the definitions in the world can never explain what God is, and no more can any amount of philosophizing explain how by His Spirit He enters into man, regenerates him or operates within him; this is a mystery more infinite than life itself, but we have not only the postulates of reason that it may be so, but the Word of God and our own experience that it is so, which is more powerful evidence than anything metaphysics could ever bring to us.

(5) Is it a definite, conscious, once-for-all experience?

Note the following expressions:

"It is a crisis done definitely, done once for all."— J. F. Carson, Evangelistic Work, Jan., 1900.

"The baptism of the Spirit is the beginning of the full Christian experience and that can never be repeated."—Cumming, "Through the Eternal Spirit," page 119.

"He must not continue praying for the baptism for that cannot be repeated."—MacNeil, "Spirit-filled Life," page 39.

"It is a definite experience of which a person may know whether or not he has it."—Torrey, "Baptism with the Spirit."

These are but a few of the many similar expressions that might be quoted from writers, all of whom are speaking of an experience subsequent to regeneration, such as is under consideration.

Certainly it is definite, an actual occurrence definitely brought to pass, else nothing to be appreciated. Definiteness does not, however, necessarily imply consciousness. The act of self-dedication, the committal to God for this filling are both definite and conscious in the believer's experience, but the filling consequent thereon may not at the moment be realized in his consciousness; the filling is a reality within him, nevertheless.

How then, it is asked, does he come into the consciousness of it? In two ways,—in three ways it may be said. I know at once this filling is mine; having met the conditions as best I can, I receive the promise of the Spirit by faith, Gal. 3: 14. I have taken God at His word and I know. This may be called one way, but note the distinction between knowledge and consciousness as here used. I know in the above sense and yet I may not have come into the consciousness of it as a realized possession, and into this consciousness I come in two ways, the more usual of which, certainly the more satisfactory, is by

His own manifestation in me and through me. As F. B. Meyer says, "Reckoning that God has kept His word with you dare to believe it, though you may not be conscious of any emotion, and you will find when you come to work or to suffer or to meet temptation that there will be in you the consciousness of a power which you have never known before, and which will indicate the filling of the Spirit."

This by no means excludes the possibility of an immediate consciousness. The fiery tongues, the sound and the shaken house are no more; the "electric waves" that seemed to go through Finney, and all such peculiar experiences are largely, if not wholly, matters of temperament; no matter how Spirit-filled some men might become, they never could approach unto anything of such character, but may, nevertheless, have the more silent, quiet witness of a feeling within as deep, as sure, as self-satisfying.

It is not our thought to speak in doubtful terms about the reality of this or the more extraordinary experiences of men like Finney, but only to affirm that such are not essential to the "filling" itself, and that the more usual way into the consciousness of it is as above denoted.

Is then this experience once for all?

Whether it be the filling in the sense of the sudden, decisive experience for some specific purpose, or whether it be the more habitual fulness of the Spirit, the answer in either case is a decided No. The fact that Scripture records many fillings in the former sense ought to be an answer sufficiently definite in the negative so far as it is concerned. *All who have claimed a distinction between the first so-called,*

never-to-be repeated experience and later fillings, have
utterly failed to show wherein the distinction consists.

That the fulness of the Spirit as the more permanent condition of the soul is a varying quantity
no one for a moment doubts; this belongs to the
rationale of the thing we are discussing. The first
departs with the occasion and its need; the second
varies according as we commit to God or assume for
ourselves the control of our life. And yet we hear of
a "crisis," of something "taking place once for all,"
and often the bewildered inquirer finds himself
confronted with a certain day of the year as marking
the exact time of this "never-to-be-repeated experience."

Cumming, whose distinction between the baptism
and the filling of the Spirit, is by no means a clear
one, speaks of a "first time," (Through the Eternal
Spirit, page 114.) Is not this, after all, the explanation? There was a time when they first consciously
made what they conceived to be a definite and full
surrender to God. In a very certain sense such a
moment did mark a crisis. That particular surrender
can, of course, never be repeated, nor ought there
ever to be occasion for any other like it, but the resulting experience to the soul was not the "filling"
in the more specific sense of equipment for some
special purpose, but the "fulness" which must be
presupposed in the case of the former and which comes
and goes according to the constancy of our abiding
truly in Him.

We deplore the tendency which would gather
about the teacher bands of earnest inquirers who look
upon him as having had some strange never-to-be-
repeated experience, the lack of which has been
crippling their own ministry, and who, when asking

how to get it, are told to do so and so; and many of them will say, "All this have we done, and yet were never conscious of this experience of which you speak," and go away in uncertainty and sorrow, while the truth may be that many of them may have been in the possession of that very something, possibly in a greater degree than the one whose experience they fain would know.

The point of discussion is, as to what occurred at the time of this definite surrender, and that is the fulness of the Spirit exactly such as he may get many times later and exactly such as he may have had in less measure in times of lesser consecration before this crisis.

This filling of the Spirit, however it be viewed, is a matter of degree. Almost every Christian, shall we say every Christian, (yes, we must), is to a degree filled with the Spirit—a degree that in some—alas many—is inappreciable; that degree increases according to our committal of ourselves to God, and in moments of such deep definite conscious surrender as have been under consideration it leaps into fulness unmeasured, gives to the Christian the mastery over self, and sends him forth in the hour of service with a power that none can stay.

This experience then viewed in either light is not a once-for-all occurrence. That there may be a crisis, a turning point in a man's spiritual life coming at the time of this first definite surrender is true, but the fulness of the Holy Spirit which comes to him then is certainly no different in nature from what to a certain though probably slight degree was always his, nor necessarily different in degree from that which will come to him whenever he puts himself in a condition to receive it.

We need the continual fulness of the Spirit, and there is but one way to get it, and but one way to keep it. Should we wander away from God and lose this priceless blessing, well-nigh altogether it may be, we will get it again if we seek it in the self-same way as before. We need also the refilling of the Spirit for service as much as ever did the apostles, and we will get it in the same way whenever the occasion calls for it.

Furthermore, as there are those who do not know the day of their regeneration, so there are those, to whose Spirit-filled condition their holy lives and works lend evidence as undeniable as ever any man showed forth, whose testimony is that they have grown into the realization of this blessed Spirit-filled condition coming to them in accordance with the same rule without their remembering any such definite, never-to-be-repeated crisis in their lives.

(6) And now we come to what is, after all, the important question. Paul said, "Be filled with the Spirit." As already explained, Paul's more immediate reference here was to living in the Spirit-filled condition, but the conditions governing the reception of the Spirit's fulness in this sense are likewise the underlying requirements for the occasional special fillings in view of some specific service to be performed. But how may I obtain this filling of the Spirit? There is one supreme condition already suggested. There are, however, certain prerequisites to this condition and which in the various answers given to the above question have likewise, and not without warrant, been called conditions. We prefer, however, to call them prerequisites, especially as they are necessarily involved in the one supreme condition to which we shall shortly refer. Two of

these prerequisites refer to the disposition of the soul, and the third to the state of the soul, while what we shall call the one condition refers to an act of the soul.

I. The first of these prerequisites is an *Intense, unselfish desire to be thus filled*. See Isa. 44: 3, where the "water" and the "Spirit" are synonymous. It is a blessing to be earnestly desired. But note this desire must be an unselfish one. "It is no part of the Spirit's work to glorify us; His great work is to glorify Christ."—Macgregor, "A Holy Life," page 136. The desire to be used may be an accursed ambition; it is only when a deep, earnest desire for the honor and glory of Jesus marks the disposition of him who covets this experience that he is coming into the place where it may be realized.

II. The second of these prerequisites, referring also to the disposition of the soul, is *Faith*. This is not the appropriating faith of Gal. 3: 14, but faith as John F. Carson has said, "to believe it is possible for you"; faith to believe that God will do it for you because He has promised it; faith, as Scofield says, (Plain Papers on the Doctrine of the Spirit, page 65) "to believe that the risen and glorified Christ is able and willing to bestow the fulness of the Spirit," and will bestow it. Faith in the appropriating sense though involved in this former can be exercised only as the filling is accomplished. See Scofield, page 65, for a clear statement of this distinction.

III. The third prerequisite, the one referring to the state of the soul, is *Emptiness*—the necessary state of any vessel that is to be filled. We have been told to be consistent, to give up sin, to be emptied, but these are the very things no man can do, but they are the very things the Holy Spirit filling a man enables him to do, and it would be quite as pertinent to ask "How may I be emptied?" A man is no farther along when he has been told of this necessary state of the soul than he was before.

With these prerequisites clearly before us it is now in order to consider the one supreme, and what may be called, inasmuch as it refers neither to a disposition or a state, but to an act of the soul, the only condition of thus receiving the Holy Spirit in the sense of in-filling. This is what has been variously called "yieldedness" (Scofield), "abandonment" (Morgan), "full surrender" (Chapman), "consecration" (Mac-Neil). These are all excellent and expressive terms. It is a whole-hearted, absolute, unqualified, com-mittal—an unconditional surrender of ourselves to God. Of course this act is definite, and as concerns the will, final, irreversible, and never to be repeated, and it is God's idea that there should never be an occasion for any other like it, but the mistake must not be made of reading the ideal into the real. When Paul says, "yield yourselves," Rom. 6: 13, and "pre-sent your bodies a living sacrifice," Rom. 12: 1, he uses the aorist—it was to be done once for all, and this certainly is what every believer does or wills to do and thinks he does when he thus deliberately gives himself to God, but that any man ever so gave him-self to God as to leave no necessity for a further giving in all his life is to the writer a thing altogether inconceivable.

Such a definite, irrevocable committal one is sup-posed to make in the first glad hour of his surrender to Christ; in fact, he says he makes it; he means it, and upon such avowal he is received into church fellowship, but as he grows in the knowledge of God he discovers that true surrender involves sacrifice which his earlier meager experience could not reveal to him, and so "from step to step, from strength to strength, from faith to faith, the life goes on growing humbler, sweeter, more surrendered, and yet ever more filled with the Holy Spirit."— Cumming, "Through the Eternal Spirit," page 241.

And there is one thing else to be considered. True, as Scofield says, (page 61), "A sacrificer under the dispensation of the law never dreamed of reasserting authority over a creature once brought to the priest," but in all such typifications there was involved and necessarily the ideal of that which was to be, even as Paul expresses the same kind of an act by the aorist tense. Indeed, some have declared it a thing altogether impossible for man to make such an ideal surrender, seeing in it nothing less than the ill-disguised teaching of perfectionism, but even admitting the possibility of surrendering in this ideal way we must distinguish between a perfect life and a perfect surrender.

The surrender is ideal, in intent at least, but as before noted, that no man, be his surrender ever so perfect came into a condition of life thereby in which he never found anything else to be surrendered, so no man, no matter how perfect his surrender, has ever been removed thereby from the possibility of the neglect of duty in some later period of his life; and to make the surrender by which a man comes into the experience under consideration something never to be repeated is practically to make it permanent, to ignore our frailty and our failures and to make no provision for the wanderer who must come back to God and receive the coveted blessing on a condition identical with that which governed its reception at the time of his first surrender.

Dr. Scofield, page 63, deplores "the practice of continually repeated consecrations (so called)," proving, as he thinks, the lack of this definite, once-for-all surrender. Certainly it is not God's idea that we should continually be doing a thing that should be done once for all, as the root meaning of consecration implies, and while possibly another word might take its place, yet since in every human nature there is still what Dr. Van Dyke in his "Gospel for an Age of Sin," calls the "radical twist" so productive of "crooked results," and since every sin is practically a taking the gift of ourselves from the altar, asserting the control of self, it is necessary whenever one is conscious of so having done, to come to God in renewed consecration; whether it be an unholy thought, a display of temper or some grosser displeasure to God it is only a difference in degree after all.

These remarks are not intended to deny that a man may have such a crisis marking day in his life from which he dates the first great filling of the Spirit, but to affirm that such a surrender is what we are supposed to make when we give ourselves to Christ, what in fact every really converted man wills to do and says he does, but which, alas for his weakness, he finds he has not done, and must either by an ever-increasing spiritual growth which involves surrender all along the way arrive, and yet be ever arriving at what is termed the "surrendered life," without the remembrance of any one particular crisal experience step into the "surrendered life," and consequently into such a fulness of the Spirit as he had never before realised, the filling of the Spirit which he then received, let it be repeated, differing only in degree from what was his in previous times; for certainly a minister who looks with rich satisfaction and rightly upon some such hour, possibly twenty years after he took upon himself the ordination vow, which in itself involves such a surrender, would not repudiate all his past life as being in no wise Spirit led, his preaching in no wise Spirit empowered, his earnest striving after holiness in no wise Spirit helped.

The filling of the Spirit we again remark is a matter of degree. Some have asked, "How much of the Spirit may I have?"

We feel like answering, "You may have all there is of Him—no more and no less," but refer the reader to the discussion elsewhere (page 66). But to have the Spirit is not to have His filling. The degree pertains to the filling; it is "evermore surrendered and evermore filled with the Holy Spirit."

What now does such surrender involve? As to service, "anything, any time, anywhere," but something else must come first—the emptiness, a heart emptied of sin and surrender implies the desire to have the heart emptied, and an effort on our part to bring it about. This effort is not, however, to be made alone—as such it were fruitless—but the Holy Spirit already within is there to help, and as the vessel is made empty and cleansed is the filling of the Spirit made possible. As Dr. Chapman ("Received ye the Holy Ghost," page 85) has said, "To give up ninety-nine parts of the nature and withhold the hundredth is to put a hindrance in the way of the blessing." After all it seems that Mr. Boys was right, "If we were asked very briefly the true meaning of being filled with the Spirit we should say that it involved not our having more of the Spirit but rather the Spirit having more of us." ("Filled with the Spirit," page 29.)

Some have made faith (Gal. 3: 4,) a condition of the filling; this, of course, is involved in the faith already mentioned, as faith to believe He will give on a certain condition involves faith to believe that He has given when that condition is met.

This is the faith that appropriates: having met the condition, reckon the thing done; wait not for any sound or coronet of flame, but go forth to live and work not trying to feel filled, but daring to believe that you are filled and that filling will become to you an experience more real than which there is none in all the universe.

Being thus filled with the Spirit the varying measure of this condition is our faithfulness; as Morgan has said, page 231, "The filling of the Spirit is retained by abiding in Christ." Acts 5: 32 and I John 3: 24, is the Bible rule for this retention. Yet we need for each separate service a new and additional equipment of power; not that all the filling has been lost, but that such equipment comes only as occasion demands; then in humble acknowledgement of any thing which may not have been as He would have it, by faith as before reckon the needed filling yours and going forth to duty let Him prove Himself unto you in power.

11

THE EMBLEMS OF THE HOLY SPIRIT

WORDS are often but lame vehicles in the conveyance of truth. Oftentimes at their best they but "half reveal and half conceal" the hidden depths of thought. To say the Holy Spirit is like the wind is to express more than many volumes can contain, and possibly just because this is so, God has chosen the use of many symbols to illustrate what otherwise, because of the poverty of our language, we could never know.

There are in the Scriptures six emblems of the Holy Spirit.

I. FIRE.

In Isa. 4: 4, He is called the "Spirit of burning," where the reference is to the purging of Jerusalem from defilement.

In Matt. 3: 11, and Luke 3: 16, of Jesus it is said, "He shall baptize you with the Holy Spirit and fire." To what does the "fire" refer?

(1) Hell-fire.—So Meyer, Lange, DeWette, Gess, Keim, Hengstenberg, Osterzee, and many others.

(2) Suffering with view of purification.—Cumming.

(3) Holy Spirit under the emblem of fire.

(a) For fiery boldness and zeal.—Farrar.

(b) For purification—Godet, Calvin, Bengel, Olshausen, Riddle, Alford, Schaff, Andrew Murray, Scofield, Morgan and many others.

Both the first and third views have much to support them. The arguments are too lengthy to be here in place. We are inclined to that which makes it an emblem of the Holy Spirit. It is hardly possible that the reference in John's words can be to the "tongues of fire" at Pentecost, though the same divine principle has for its emblem there a visible manifestation of what is here expressed in word. If such reference were in mind, the primary signification of the emblem as here used would at least be changed, for, certainly apart from such reference, if the emblem refer at all to the Holy Spirit, the primary thought as conceived by nearly all expositors must be to His purifying influences. Fire is a separator— a purifier; we are counselled to buy gold refined by fire, Rev. 3: 18, so the Holy Spirit, the fire of God, purifies the soul by consuming everything in it out of harmony with the divine kingdom.

(4) In Luke 12: 49 Jesus says, "I came to cast fire upon the earth. Morgan, supported by abundant critical authority, refers the fire in this passage to the pentecostal effusion of the Holy Spirit.

The desire of the Son of God following the statement would seem to confirm this view; however, the immediate reference to division, the natural and wise avoidance of imported meaning, and the equally consistent interpretation of the desire would seem to favor the opinion of Meyer, Alford, Lange, and others, that the thought in mind was the spiritual excitement and discord consequent upon the proclamation of the Gospel.

(5) In Acts 2: 3, it is recorded that there appeared unto them "tongues like as of fire." While the tongue had immediate reference to the instrument of service

to be employed, the fiery appearance is taken by common consent as emblematic of the Spirit with distinct reference to His inspirational work and consequent zeal and ardor of the disciples in the undertaking before them.

II. WIND.

The Holy Spirit is so revealed in three different places.

(1) In Ezk. 37: 7–10, occurs the reanimation of the dry bones through the agency of the Spirit of God where chiefly His vivifying power is set forth.

(2) John 3: 8, with reference to His regenerative work as indicative of His mysterious, independent, irresistible, penetrating, vivifying and purifying influence.

(3) In Acts 2: 2, "a sound as of the rushing of a mighty wind" filled the house—indicative here of His mighty unseen power. The tongues were seen, the wind was heard, but neither was felt. Neither flame nor wind was a reality. The tongue of light resembled fire; the sound was only compared to that of a mighty rushing wind. Notice also that the house in Acts 4: 31 was shaken.

III. WATER.

(1) In Ex. 17: 6, we see Moses in obedience to divine instruction smiting a rock in the wilderness, and out of it came flowing water pure and fresh, of which the thirsty Israelites drank and were satisfied. That rock was Christ, I Cor. 10: 4, smitten for us, and that water life-giving and refreshing, the Spirit, poured out on the ground of his accomplished work.

(2) In Ezk. 36: 25–27, the people are to be sprinkled with clean water, a new heart and spirit given unto them and His Spirit put within them; the reality of that which was typified in Num. 19, and referring beyond doubt to the converting and sanctifying influences of the Holy Spirit.

(3) In Ezk. 47: 1, the prophet in a vision sees a river of water flowing out from the temple running through the desert carrying life wherever it goes and healing at length the waters of the sea whither it flows. With this connect I Cor. 6: 19 and Jno. 7: 38–39.

(4) In John 3: 5 is mentioned the birth "of water and of the Spirit." Here again water is symbolic of the Spirit. No matter whether the water be referred to Old Testament washings (Smeaton, Lampe); to John's baptism or to Christian baptism these all have the same underlying idea,—they are symbolic representations of purification from sin. So also Tit. 3: 5.

(5) In John 4: 14, the Holy Spirit, according to Smeaton, Riddle, Lange, Calvin, Luthardt, Keil, is promised as a well of water springing up into ever-lasting life. This phrase is referred by Justin and Cyprian to baptism; by Olshausen to Jesus Himself; by Meyer to the truth; by Tholuck and Weiss to the word of salvation; by Grotius to the evangelical doctrine; by Lucke to faith; by Westcott and Godet to eternal life itself.

(6) In John 7: 38–39, it is said, "If any man thirst let him come to me and drink," and that out of the believer should flow "rivers of living water," and while it is not said the Holy Spirit is the river, but only that such remarks were made with reference to the Holy Spirit ("this spake he of the Spirit") that

is, the Holy Spirit was the agent and principle of the great outflowing streams of Christian influence and testimony, yet as the Holy Spirit is the inner fountain there is full propriety in finding in the passage an emblematic reference to Him as a satisfying, transforming and life-giving power.

IV. SEAL.

He is thus revealed three times. See chapter on the "Sealing of the Spirit." The Holy Spirit as a seal makes the believer secure as the property of God, works an assurance of such security in the believer's heart, Rom. 8: 16, bringing to him a consequent comfort and feeling of rest, transforming him into the likeness of Jesus, whose very image is on the seal and making this life a heaven, for as an earnest He has given Himself to us here with all that He brings as a foretaste of the coming inheritance of glory.

V. OIL.

Two hundred and two times in the Word the anointing with oil is referred to, in eighty-eight of which references the word oil in some form is mentioned. In addition to this, the word oil occurs ninety-nine times and the word ointment thirty-one times. We must be warned, however, against endeavoring to see in every such usage a prefiguration of the Holy Spirit and His work, as some without warrant do. Of many of these passages such reference is true; the immediate references in Scripture to the Holy Spirit as oil must, however, be gathered from the five passages in which He is spoken of as anointing three of these, Luke 4: 18; Acts 4: 27; 10: 38, refer to the anointing of Jesus, and the other two,

I John 2: 20, 27 and II Cor. 1: 21, referring to the Holy Spirit as an anointing for the believer.

There are four Scriptural uses of anointing: (1) Anointing the guest, Eccl. 7: 1; 9: 8; Prov. 27: 9; Luke 7: 46. (2) Anointing for burial, Matt. 26: 12; John 12: 3, 7. (3) Anointing for healing, Isa. 1: 6; Jer. 8: 22; Luke 10: 34; Mark 6: 13; Jas. 5: 14. (4) Anointing for separation unto a holy calling, Ex. 29: 7; 30: 23, 33. Every believer is a king and priest unto God, and for his holy life and vocation is set apart by the anointing received at regeneration. The ointment was always charged with a sweet perfume; the odor of Mary's ointment filled all the room, and when the High Priest came forth his garments anointed with holy oil, shed a rich fragrance all about him. When describing the beauty of the character of Jesus, the inspired poet said, "All thy garments smell of Myrrh and Aloes and Cassia " and so the Christian who has the anointing from the Holy One is to be recognized by the sweet fragrance of holy character, the life that is redolent with holy and heavenly influence.

There are eleven passages in the Bible connecting oil with light, Ex. 25: 6; 27: 20; 35: 8, 14, 28; 39: 37; Num. 4: 9, 16; Lev. 24: 2; Zech. 4: 2–12; Matt. 25: 3–6. The first eight are plain statements concerning the oil for the tabernacle light which is according to Old Testament typology taken by an almost common consent as a prefiguration of the Holy Spirit.

In Zech. 4: 2–12. Zerubbabel confronted with a mountain of hindrance is taught by the vision of a candle-stick fed by two inexhaustible ducts of oil from living olive trees, that the hindrance should be removed by the Spirit of the Lord; so the church is a bearer of light whose function is that of illumination for which it depends wholly upon its supply of oil from God which is His Spirit.

In Matt. 25: 3-6, the oil in the lamps, as Stier (Words of Jesus, Vol. 3, page 311), has said, "is according to the general symbology of Scripture the Holy Spirit who nourishes the flame of life in the heart which without Him holds merely a dry extinguished wick in the bowl." Such reference of the oil, as here used, to the Holy Spirit, is in accordance with the common consensus of opinion. Oil is an illuminator and so is the flame of spiritual life kindled within and kept burning by the oil of the Spirit illuminating the conscience and dispelling the moral darkness of the heart, shining out into the world through the light of Christian character unto the glory of the Christian's Father, Matt. 5: 16.

The Oil of Joy.

This expression in Isa. 61: 3, derives its significance from the custom of festive anointings at entertainments, Ps. 23: 5, and on occasions of great rejoicing. So in Ps. 104: 15, we read of "oil to make the face shine," but whether oil in such connection is ever used with figurative reference to the Holy Spirit is a question admitting of no certain solution. There is one passage in Heb. 1: 9, declaring that Jesus was "anointed with the oil of gladness above his fellows"; this "oil of gladness" Smeaton, Cumming, Chapman, refer to the Holy Spirit, but this is in no wise certain. It refers to his exaltation, joy, the anointing being the setting apart to His kingly office (Stewart), or, which is more to be preferred, the crowning of the Sovereign with joy as at a royal banquet (Westcott, Olshausen) and by scarcely a modern exegete is referred to the Holy Spirit, while many stoutly combat any such allusion; for instance, Meyer says,

"The sense of the author is departed from when the fathers and early expositors interpret the expression of the anointing of the Son by the Holy Spirit"; and Olshausen says, "The anointing with oil of joy is not to be understood of the anointing to the office of king or prophet, or even of the anointing with the Holy Spirit in general, but the figurative expression is derived from the well-known custom of anointing the head at festivals."

We do know that the Holy Spirit is the Spirit of joy, Gal. 5: 22; Eph. 5: 18, 19; I Thes. 1: 6; and the author of all spiritual gladness and no figure could be more appropriately applied to Him than the "oil of gladness," but that such is the reference in the passage before us is hardly to be maintained.

VI. DOVE.

The Holy Spirit is so revealed once. In each of the gospels, Matt. 3: 16; Mark 1: 10; Luke 3: 22; John 1: 32, it is mentioned that the Holy Spirit in bodily shape, like a dove descended from Heaven and sat upon Jesus while He was praying. Whether before the time of Christ the dove was regarded as a symbol of the Holy Spirit is a question of much interest. The dove of Noah's ark and of Solomon's Song are conceived to be types of the church; among the Syrians the dove was considered as emblem of the fructifying powers of nature, and accordingly we find the Talmud translating in Gen. 1: 2, "The Spirit of God like a dove brooded over the waters." In Cant. 2: 12, it is said, "The voice of the dove is the voice of the Spirit." But at the Lord's baptism the Holy Spirit by descending in bodily shape, like a dove upon Jesus, established that gentle creature ever after as an emblem of Himself.

Think of the many beautiful characteristics of a dove. How lovely was the character of Jesus because of those dove-like traits, sweet-tempered and gentle, yet just like Him may we be. There is gentleness, tenderness, loveliness, innocence, mildness, peace, purity, patience—all this and more for him in whose heart is made a place for the dove-like Spirit to nestle.

12

THE RESISTANCE OF THE HOLY SPIRIT

UNDER the above phrase standing as the title of this chapter it has seemed wise to class all the sins against the Holy Spirit. We make a mistake in limiting the scope of a word by a solitary use of it in Scripture. A true theory must above all represent a consistent philosophy. Dr. Chapman ("Life of Blessing," page 79), and Dr. Morgan ("Spirit of God," page 237), have said that only the unregenerate resist the Holy Spirit, presumably because the only mention of resisting the Holy Spirit, where the word resist is used, refers to the unregenerate; but certainly there is no way to sin against the Holy Spirit either by the Christian or the unbeliever, save by resisting Him.

So it is said only the Christian can grieve Him, presumably because the only mention of grieving the Holy Spirit, where the word grieve is used, refers to the believer; but surely the tender, loving heart of God is grieved by the stubborn resistance of the unregenerate. It is hardly wise to go through Scripture on such straight lines making divisions and establishing theories on the single use of an individual word. With this precaution the several phrases setting forth the sins against the Holy Spirit may now be examined.

1. Resisting the Spirit. Used only once and of

unregenerate persons, Acts 7: 51. It consists in the resistance of the will to the purpose of the Spirit of God as manifested in His influence and His work. "There is an element," says Cumming, page 270, "even in a Christian, which often, if not always, is found in the same attitude against the Holy Spirit." He quotes, and rightly, Gal. 5: 17. It is impossible to divorce the Ego from the sinful principle still within the Christian, and whenever this struggle goes on, even before the better side has gained the victory, and especially when, alas, the evil side does, there is certainly a resistance to the will and work of the Holy Spirit.

2. Grieving the Spirit. Used only once and of Christians, Eph. 4: 30. It means "to make sorrowful," discovers His personality and reveals His tenderness. "It is not strange," says Scofield, (Plain Papers on the Doctrine of the Spirit, page 54,) "that some have found here the mother part of the divine love." The immediate reference is to corrupt speech, as is shown by the context and the close connecting Greek particle "and," but of course the truth must admit of a wider reference, "Whenever He is thwarted," says Morgan, (Spirit of God, page 242,) "whenever He is disobeyed, whenever He gives some new revelation of the Christ which brings no response, He is grieved." In Isa. 63: 10, the Holy Spirit is said to have been "vexed," as if he had become angry and this thought, Cumming, (Through the Eternal Spirit, page 271), prefers as that embodied in the original. Indeed, the Septuagint renders it "made angry." Ps. 78: 40, however, can hardly be quoted (Cumming) in confirmation of above rendering, if we keep in mind the personality of the Holy Spirit as distinct from God.

Although anger is closely connected with the thought resident in the word, as in Gen. 34: 7, the form of the verb in Isa. 63: 10 (Piel), demands the meaning "to cause acute pain," in which there is prominent the thought of "grieving," I Ki. 1: 6; I Chron. 4: 10, and in fact the Revised Version so translates. If the idea of vexing in the sense of making angry be excluded from the word as used in the passage before us it is noteworthy that nowhere in the Word is such a frame of disposition ascribed to the Holy Spirit; tender and loving, He may be grieved, but not angered. Can He be grieved away? By the unregenerate He can in the sense that the Holy Spirit forever ceases to plead with him for a place in his heart. It is then that a man has passed beyond the limit of resistance, that unseen line which Dr. J. Addison Alexander has called "The hidden boundary between God's patience and His wrath." But the regenerate He never leaves.

3. Quenching the Spirit, I Thes. 5: 19, used only once and of Christians. It is a metaphorical expression for putting out a fire. It is impossible by candid exegesis to confine this to any one manifestation of the Holy Spirit. The most probable reference is to "prophesying," as noted in the verse following, that is, to the gift for service. We quench Him when we refuse to do His bidding; when we attempt service without waiting upon Him; when timidity keeps us from speaking the truth in response to His bidding. We cannot, however, thus limit the meaning of the injunction as does Dr. Morgan, (Spirit of God, page 244.) Of this particular reference in I Thes., exegesis makes us nowise certain, and even if it did, the phrase would not necessarily be limited thereby. The "tongue of fire," Acts 2: 3, was the symbol of

power for service, but there was also a "baptism of fire," Matt. 3: 11, conceived by many as the Holy Spirit given for purification, and in Isa. 4: 4, as conceived by many, (Smeaton, the "Doctrine of the Holy Spirit," page 32; Scofield, Plain Papers on the Doctrine of the Spirit, page 57,) He is called the "Spirit of burning," as a purifier, and both power for service and purity of life are effected by the presence and effort of the Holy Spirit within us. This would all be true even were no such figures used in the word. "To quench the Spirit, therefore, is to resist this twofold work of purification and of use," Scofield, page 57. The quenching of the Spirit may properly be said to be an offence limited to the Christian.

4. Tempting the Spirit. The word "tempt" in this passage is better translated "try" or "test." It comes from "peirazo" and has a two-fold meaning.

(I). To try, to put to the test.

  (a) God tests men, Heb. 11: 17.
  (b) Men test God, Acts 15: 10 and 5: 9.
  (c) Men test themselves, II Cor. 13: 5.
  (d) Men test each other.

(II). To tempt to sin. This is the work of the Evil One. God tempts no man, neither can He be tempted, Jas. 1: 13. Peter said Ananias lied to the Holy Spirit, Acts 5: 3. He also says in the ninth verse they agreed to "test" the Holy Spirit. Now without any thought of the Holy Spirit they may have agreed to lie to Peter, and Peter filled with the Holy Spirit, being His bearer and organ, rightly interpreted the attempted deception as practised not upon himself but upon the Spirit.

But since Peter, in verse nine, says they agreed together to test the Holy Spirit and such conception implies a conscious act and deliberate purpose, and since so manifest was the Spirit's presence and power through the gift of discernment and tongues and physical manifestations, that the most thoughtless could not but be aware of His presence and of His power as resting especially upon the apostles, and the possibility of His discovering to them the proposed deception would therefore naturally occur to them; it is certainly the more probable solution of the occurrence, however, Peter's statement may be explained, to conclude that with the primal purpose of possibly gaining an enviable reputation or securing a maintenance (what it was must be conjectured) they planned to deceive Peter, which thing involved a testing of the Holy Spirit to which they deliberately gave themselves. Cumming, (Through the Eternal Spirit, page 273,) says they tempted the Holy Spirit "to desert the church as His dwelling place and resign His task," but hardly in this sense can the Holy Spirit be tempted.

Nowhere is it said that we tempt the Holy Spirit as that expression is construed by language or usage. There is mentioned, however, the sin of testing the Holy Spirit or God, distrusting His infinite perfections and putting Him to the test of our dispositions and actions. In the case of Ananias and Sapphira it consisted primarily in testing His omniscience and His operation whether He would know of the deception and reveal it to Peter. Can the Christian test the Holy Spirit?

Ananias doubted His punishment (whether the Holy Spirit would discover the deception or do anything if He did); Christians have distrusted His readiness to bless. Ananias tested the former, which was a sinful thing to do; Christians test the latter, which is certainly a good thing to do. Prove Me, test Me, He says. Test then has a two-fold meaning. It is doubtful whether a Christian ever tests God in the evil sense. Were Ananias and Sapphira Christians? Augustine and a multitude of others say, Yes. As many more say, No. Nobody knows, but if they were, their case could hardly argue anything for Christian experience today, as spiritual manifestations do not today furnish the same opportunity. The unregenerate test Him always, chiefly by distrusting His warning to leave them, upon continued resistance, in the hands of God for punishment, thus counting upon the long forbearance of God that He will save them in spite of their sin.

From the above it is plain there is a difference between lying to the Holy Spirit and testing the Holy Spirit, though both may belong to the same act. We may be said to lie to the Holy Spirit in a sense similar to that of Ananias in so much as we practise deception upon the church or upon the believer indwelt as they are by the Spirit. Though to the Christian it may not at the time so appear nor be thought of as intentionally directed against the Holy Spirit, yet in reality his sin has been not so much against the Spirit filled man, as it has been against the Spirit filling the man. Certainly the Holy Spirit is grieved by all such resistance to His holy will.

5. Defiling the temple of the Spirit. A temple classically means "the dwelling place of a Deity." The word is used twice in connection with the Holy Spirit, I Cor. 3: 16, 17, and 6: 19, the former referring to the church—to Christians in their organized capacity and the latter to the Christian in his

individual capacity. As by the Shechinah God dwelt in and sanctified the Jewish temple so by His Spirit He indwells and sanctifies the Christian temple.

The word "defile," I Cor. 3: 16, is the same as "destroy" in the same verse, and means "to bring into a worse state," "to mar," "to injure" and then "destroy." In the Old Testament any neglect of the temple, any desecration of it was considered as destroying it. We defile the temple of the Holy Spirit in its organized capacity (the church), in all the church strife and division, (this is the primal reference in this third chapter of I Cor.), and in any perversion from its God intended use. In 6: 19, "fornication" as a sin against the body is under consideration, which body Paul calls a "temple of the Holy Spirit," inasmuch as the body is the vehicle and tabernacle of the human spirit which is indwelt by the Spirit of God. We sin against the body as God's temple through every form of bodily abuse. In both these instances we are resisting and grieving the Holy Spirit.

As the lie, Acts 5: 3, need not necessarily be construed as directed deliberately against the Holy Spirit (it is impossible to analyze the minds of the sinning pair), so may the sins against the temple be likewise considered. But as Peter, because filled with the Holy Spirit and acting for the Holy Spirit, construed the lie not as to him but in reality to the Holy Spirit, so sin against the Spirit inhabited temple (church or believer), may be called, in fact must be, a sin against the Holy Spirit, even though, as in the case of the lie, the offending one may not have consciously so directed it.

6. Despising the Spirit, Heb. 10: 29. A sin described by a word not elsewhere found in the New

Testament. Literally, it meant to insult. It is used here as designating that insult and outrage offered to that blessed Spirit through whom all divine influences are conveyed to men. It here, Heb. 10: 29, refers to the sin of apostasy and is used in connection with the disposition and actions of those who, as elsewhere described, Heb. 6: 4, 5, were once enlightened, and made partakers of the Holy Ghost, tasted of the heavenly gift, of the good word of God and the powers of the age to come.

By many scholars this sin has been made identical with the blasphemy against the Spirit as set forth in the Gospels. In a certain sense this is true, both arising from the same disposition of soul and both referring to a high degree of insolent and determined opposition to the wondrous unfolding and most manifest working of the Holy Spirit's power. A difference, however appears in the character of the sinning subjects, the sin described in the Gospels being that of those who from the beginning had malignantly set themselves to oppose the divine power as manifested in the Son of God, the latter, as we have seen, being that of those who had to a high degree received His grace and acknowledged the truth of the Spirit's teaching. While the former, as often observed, is more malignant in its manifestation; the latter, considering the position and knowledge to which they had attained and the divine influences they had enjoyed, seems scarcely less diabolical. How solemn then is the warning of the apostle against the commission of this awful crime, with which he brings the paragraph to a close, "It is a fearful thing to fall into the hands of the living God."

7. Blasphemy of the Spirit. The Unpardonable Sin. What is it? Who shall presume to say? Did

not the Master leave it shrouded in certain mystery?
We present herewith in clear outline the different
opinions and such evidence as would seem to justify
what to the writer appears the safest interpretation
of Scripture as it bears on the solemn investigation
before us.

In Matt. 12: 31, 32, the Saviour says, "Wherefore
I say unto you every sin and blasphemy shall be
forgiven unto men; but the blasphemy against the
Holy Spirit shall not be forgiven unto men. And whosoever speaketh a word against the Son of Man, it
shall be forgiven him, but whosoever speaketh
against the Holy Spirit it shall not be forgiven him,
neither in this world nor in the world to come." In
Mark 3: 28–30, it is also written, "Verily I say unto
you, All sins shall be forgiven unto the sons of men
and the blasphemies wherewithsoever they blaspheme;
but he that shall blaspheme aga'nst the Holy Spirit
hath never forgiveness but is guilty of eternal sin;
because they said, He hath an unclean Spirit"; and
in Luke 12: 10, is found, "And whosoever shall
speak a word against the Son of Man it shall be
forgiven him; but unto him that blasphemeth against
the Holy Spirit it shall not be forgiven."

Before adverting to the different interpretations
certain helpful observations and distinctions may
properly and with profit be noticed here.

(1) Every sin is a sin against the Holy Spirit
though far from approaching the nature of this one
inexpiable sin which Jesus calls blasphemy against
the Spirit. The name "Sin against the Spirit" is
therefore open to misunderstanding and should give
place to the proper designation used by Jesus.

(2) The word translated "blasphemy" (either from
βλάπτω, to injure, and φήμη speech; or from βλάξ,

braggart, stupid, and φήμη speech), originally means malicious speaking against sacred things, and is used of different degrees of sinning, up to the blasphemy of Jehovah in the Old Testament and the Holy Spirit in the New.

(3) Jesus evidently had in mind the unpardonable offense of the Old Testament dispensation where in Lev. 24: 16, it is stated (R. V.), "He that blasphemeth the name of the Lord shall surely be put to death." Under this law Stephen was stoned, but by so much is the grace of the New Testament dispensation superior that blasphemy against God shall be forgiven, yea, He even goes on to say that he who "speaketh against" the Son of Man shall be forgiven, but the speaking against the Holy Spirit—such blasphemy but sounds the sinner's eternal doom.

We see no objection, therefore to Olshausen's distinction of three degrees in the sin of blasphemy; that against the Father, against the Son and against the Holy Spirit. But to find the ground for such gradation in the relative ranks of the three persons in the Godhead is entirely without warrant. By such arrangement the Father would stand the lowest in the Trinity. The aggravation of the crime is determined not by the rank of the object blasphemed, but by the added clearness of the revelation of God given to man through the revelation of the Spirit, in proportion to which the sin is all the more conscious and determined.

It is safe to say the view which makes this sin possible only when Christ was visibly present among men (Menken, Jerome, Chrysostom), has little, if anything, in its favor. Saul was a blasphemer, I Tim. 1: 13, and the Jews crucified Jesus after the resurrection of Lazarus, but they did it in the ignorance of unbelief. Saul was pardoned and of the Jews Jesus said, "Father, forgive them, they know not what they do"; but the more comprehensive and convincing the "greater works," John 14: 12, of this day, the more powerful the convictions of the Spirit who was to come in such capacity after Christ, the less possible does the plea of ignorance become and the more possible the terrible crime in question. The unpardonable sin, Stier has well said, is "preeminently the sin of the last time."

With these observations before us we now inquire into the nature of the sin itself.

The various explanations, while differing much in their specific interpretation, are, after all, as we hope to make clear, but the emphasis of different sides of the same truth. They may be arranged under two general heads.

1. Those which make it some definite thing the sinner has done.

2. Those which make it a state of soul to which he has arrived. Let us now analyze these two views. The first may again be conveniently divided as follows:

(1) Those making it one particular sin, as ascribing the miracle of Jesus to Satan. That this is the sin, Wesley declares "nothing is more clear in the Bible." Since the days of miracles are past, says Broadus, therefore the unpardonable sin can no longer be committed. Christ, however, did not say the Pharisees had committed this sin, and the most that can be positively argued is that their conduct proved them well on the way toward it. Mark 3: 30 does not necessarily impute the sin unto them. "Because they said He had an unclean Spirit," may be simply the ground on which He based the warning. However, though this be true, we are inclined to believe with

Meyer, Broadus, Delitzsch and others, that they did commit the sin in question, though this, of course, must remain doubtful. That they could be warned against it is to some (Stier, Lange, Chadwick), argument they had not committed it; but could not those solemn words have sounded their doom as well as warned them of impending danger? To some Christ's prayer on the cross argues they had not committed it; it is said that if the crucifiers with all their evidence from a three years' ministry knew not what they were doing, scarcely could these who thus far had only eighteen months of it. It does not appear, and yet the instance before us had its peculiar aggravations, while even Christ's last prayer could have its general reference without including some, even many, who stood within the sound of it. However, if this allegation of the Pharisees was an instance of the sin in question, how does it follow with Wesley that it can be "this and nothing more?" Might this not have been but one instance of it? The occasion made this utterance the natural expression of their wicked hearts, but could not the same sinful disposition have prompted and prompt today other utterances just as heinous, and so leave the soul subject to the same fearful condemnation? The blasphemous utterance was the occasion of the Saviour's fearful declaration; it was, we are strongly inclined to believe, an instance of this most fearful of crimes, but that such crime must be confined to this one particular ascription we can gather no semblance of worthy proof from the pages of Scripture.

(2) Another shade of opinion under the same general view is that the sin consists in any blasphemous utterance of sufficient malignity and

heinousness to deserve the condemnation given it by the Saviour. This is certainly an advance over the preceding opinion; it has not only in its favour equally with the other the derivative meaning of blasphemy (a malicious verbal utterance), but also the almost universal concession that blasphemy against the Spirit is not something directed against the Spirit personally. The Jews had no thought of malice against the Holy Spirit; it was all directed against Christ. Why should it be any more harmful to speak a word against the Spirit than to speak against either of the other persons of the Godhead? It is not the rank of the Person, but the increased clearness of revelation as furnished by the Spirit, in the face of which a man knowingly and wilfully sins that aggravates the crime and makes it unpardonable. Blasphemy against God and the Son of Man is pardonable, but blasphemy against the Father or the Son is also unpardonable, if committed under the above noticed conditions, for by that very fact it becomes blasphemy against the Spirit.

That the blasphemy must, however, according to the etymology of the word, manifest itself in some verbal expression is the distinguishing characteristic of the present opinion, and the condition which J. J. Owen and others have made imperative to its correct interpretation.

(3) There is yet a third shade of opinion belonging to this same general view, namely, that this sin is any act verbal or otherwise of equal malignity and heinousness with such utterances as have been under consideration. This has the etymology of the word blasphemy against it. The Saviour said it was injurious speaking against the Spirit that was unpardonable, and a rigid consistency with the

letter would compel us at once to reject the opinion now before us. It is not unreasonable to suppose that every malicious and wilful opposer of Christ will manifest his opposition in verbal expression, and all other cases of unpardonable sinning noted in the Word may, we believe, be seen at least to include such manifestation; but is such strict adherence to the letter either necessary or wise? Certainly deeds are as damnable as words and dispositions as contemptible as verbal expressions, and with certain propriety we may speak of a man's conduct being blasphemous as well as anything he might say. Thus we hear Whedon, Oettinger and others declaring that blasphemy may as truly be committed in thought or in act as in speech, and may rather be defined as the offering a presumptuous insult to God.

The arguments in favor of the first general view are:

I. The Saviour's words undoubtedly had particular reference to something the Pharisees did.

II. He expressly said that doing something (speaking against the Holy Spirit), was the Unpardonable Sin.

III. In a very certain sense it is a thing done, a word expressed, a deed committed, a thought entertained that must be subject or not to divine clemency. If by a state expositors mean a condition of soul, this God would have remedied but not forgiven.

If now the first general view be accepted, the first shade of opinion under it we decidedly reject; the second is favored by the etymology of the word; the third, which includes the other two, is favored by the very nature of sin in general, by the spirit rather than the letter of the term blasphemy and by reasonable inference from all other Scripture bearing upon

the sin in question. If the sin, therefore, be understood as something done, the last mentioned opinion
is decidedly preferable. A final conclusion, however,
must be reserved until we have examined the other
general view, namely, that the blasphemy of the
Holy Spirit is a state of soul to which the man by
repeated sinning has arrived. Here mention should
be made of the opinion of Augustin who made the
sin in question to be "Final Independence." This
was the view also of Guthrie and of Chalmers, and
is held by a few today. With this view Prof. Smeaton
of Edinburg coincides. It is, however, strenuously
opposed by the vast majority of modern scholars.
What is it but the substitution of a foregone conclusion
for the disposition that made it inevitable?

To this second general class belongs Calvin, and
following him almost uniformly the Reformed
divines who make this state to be one of wilful and
malicious opposition to the most convincing evidence
as furnished by the Holy Spirit. A few of the
definitions that may properly be classed here are as
follows: Riddle,—"A state of wilful determined
opposition in the presence of light to the power of
the Holy Spirit, virtually a moral suicide, a killing
of the conscience so that the human spirit is absolutely
insusceptible to the influences of the Holy Spirit."
Oosterzee,—"Conscious and stubborn hatred against
God and that which is divine as it exists in its highest
development." Stier,—"We regard the Unpardonable Sin,—of which Christ was led to speak from a
special occasion so that He characterized it according
to one of its expressions—not merely in this or that
other of its manifold expressions, but in its deepest
ground—it is the rejection of the perfectly known,
immediate testimony of the Spirit developed

in a human being till it brings him to the same nature with Satan." Oettingen,—"Perpetual impenitence and incredulity even to the end, which from a rebellious and most obstinate repudiation of the testimony of the Holy Spirit manifesting Himself in the Gospel and working in the hearts of men confess to light set forth through word and deed in blaspheming the Holy Spirit."

Now what is meant by the state of the soul? We have used the term soul as the more general and designative of the psychical man to which the powers of the mind and heart appertain. We speak of the state of a man's health; the state of his body,—sound or unsound; and so we speak of the state of a man's soul as being one of spiritual insusceptibility, dead and incapable of spiritual impression. This state or condition of the soul may properly be distinguished from the principle of sin within the man; it is resultant condition of the unrestrained operation of that principle, and like the principle is not subject to divine pardon. God never forgives principles; He never forgives a state as just conceived; it must be subject to cure rather than to pardon. The principle of sin (sin in its root) in a man manifests itself first in simple indifference to the claims and strivings of the Spirit (what Nitzsch calls "passive neutrality"); this might be called the defensive attitude, simply resisting the Spirit. In some cases certain elements and conditions contrive to change this indifference into an active opposition; the principle of sin no longer merely resists but begins to oppose; it takes up an offensive attitude and as this active antagonism increases, growing more confirmed and more hateful with advancing years, the soul hardens and as a consequence of it loses its religious susceptibility, which condition marks the limit toward which every unconverted man is tending and beyond which he can not go and be in a savable condition. It is that

> "—— bourne by us unseen,
> By which each path is crossed,
> Beyond which God Himself hath sworn
> That he who goes is lost."

Herein is one way of conceiving of the state of the soul, but may we not with equal propriety conceive of this condition as productive of the outward expression whereby the inner disposition becomes manifest to the world? In fact, so most expositors speak of it. Attempt has been made to distinguish between the state of the soul as a condition and a disposition. This may be done, but it tends rather to obscure than to clarify and involves the inquirer himself in a state of psychological confusion. In the last analysis the hardened condition of the soul is nothing less nor more than the disposition of confirmed obdurateness. It is the hardened mind that antagonizes, the hardened heart that hates what is divine, and when we speak of religious insusceptibility, we can properly mean nothing more than one characteristic of the inner man to whom such state of soul pertains. It at once becomes evident therefore that whether we speak of the Unpardonable Sin as an act or as a state of sin it is but one or the other of two ways of referring to the same thing. The former defines the sin in terms of the fruit of the tree; the latter defines it in terms of the tree itself. (Matt. 12: 33, 34.)

Although in Christ's solemn declaration there may have been and doubtless was the intentional reference to an individual actual sin, it is plain that as such it could not exist save as the veriest acme of a sinful development of what Julius Muller calls "an accumulated degeneracy of the moral condition," for certainly says this same scholar in his profound work on the "Christian Doctrine of Sin," page 476, Vol. II, "this sin is not a merely outward act, as if by the secret magic of certain words which do not emanate from the depths of the heart, one could commit the worst sin and consign himself immediately to eternal perdition."

In view of all which, it must be clear that it is the condition of the man rather than any action that makes his case hopeless, and that therefore it must be in respect to this crime as all others, as Stier has well said, "the internal sin as such that is judged, though apprehended and convicted in its expression." The above distinction is of course necessary in any attempted analysis of the sin in question, or any other sin, but that in definition it should result in defining the sin in one aspect to the exclusion of the other is not only unnecessary, but unfortunate and unwise. Delitzsch has expressed himself in a way that ought to meet with entire approval. He says, "It is not the individual word of blasphemy itself, or the individual deed of blasphemous opposition, but these taken in connection with the disposition of mind which is manifested in them, that constitutes the Unpardonable Sin."

Whether forgiveness would be denied, if craved, is a useless inquiry, since the sin is unpardonable not on God's account, but on the sinner's account, for he is, as Riddle says, "virtually a moral suicide," having forever killed his conscience and destroyed his religious susceptibility and removed himself from the possibility of ever asking forgiveness. Repentance is the gift of God and the unpardonable sinner has driven from him the only person who could ever work repentance in his heart.

Another question of the present investigation pertains to the more exact nature of the disposition which drew upon it the fearful judgment of Christ. It was not only that of confirmed resistance to the Spirit as we have tried to show, but a malicious and hateful antagonism of the Spirit, (Muller, Stier, Grashof, Calvin). Such certainly is to be gathered from all other passages descriptive of the sin, and such certainly was the disposition of the blaspheming Jews in the Gospels. It was as Stier has said, "the consummated sin of the devil." Their repudiation of the Christ was made in the presence of the clearest light; but to have acknowledged this man to be the Christ would have been to repudiate their past and to have sacrificed their cause, and this with diabolical meanness they resolved they would not do. They will escape the necessity of believing; deny the fact (the cure) they cannot; interpret it they will; they will ascribe it to the power of the devil. False and absurd, hateful and hellish, but what matter, let Judaism be saved be the consequence what it may! ! ! ! It was an opposition that was conscious, determined, prolonged, hateful—a voluntary closing their eyes to the most abundant light and this with most malicious intent.

Grasping the blasphemy of the Holy Spirit, therefore, for its complete characterization both in the tree and the fruit thereof, Matt. 12: 33, 34, and still in harmony with Christ's apprehension of it in one of its expressions, we would define the Unpardonable Sin as the blasphemous manifestation in word or deed of an internal state of soul to which a man has

arrived by a continued resistance and increasing
opposition to the clearest and most undoubted
revelation of God's Spirit, which state when once
attained, is one of contemptuous and malicious hatred
of all that pertains to the Son of God and which
by its very nature is bound to manifest itself as
such.

With this we believe a fair exegesis of all other
passages relating to this sin will agree. Since the
Saviour said that all other sins but this were pardonable, it is at once evident that all other cases of fatal
sinning mentioned in the word must be identical and
harmonious with the one of which the Saviour
speaks (so most authority), I John 5:16; II Tim. 3:
8; Jude 12: 13; Heb. 6: 4–8; 10: 26–31.

Two questions remain for brief notice. The first
is, Who commits the blasphemy against the Holy
Spirit? Some answer, "The regenerate only." But
if the Jews to whom Jesus spoke concerning this sin
were guilty of it, as we are inclined to believe, to
what a destructive enervation of the idea contained
in the new birth must this opinion lead. Even if they
did not commit it, the mere fact that as unregenerate
men they could be warned as well on the way toward
it is entirely subversive of the opinion just expressed.
Others, while admitting what is beyond doubt the
fact, that the unregenerate commit the sin, also urge
the opinion that it may be committed by the regenerate, and employ in defense of their position the
passages in Heb. 6: 4–8; 10: 26–31, as descriptive
of the once regenerate. These passages in Hebrews
refer to apostasy, the way to which lay through the
sin we have been discussing; this we may maintain
beyond a reasonable doubt, but as to the former
character of the persons described we find ourselves

confronted with the never-to-be-settled question so long disputed by the chief schools of theological thought; the Calvinistic on the one side and the Lutheran and Armenian on the other. Into this question it is not the purpose of these pages to enter. The unregenerate, and we are inclined to think only the unregenerate, may commit the Unpardonable Sin.

The other question is, Will a proper understanding of the blasphemy against the Holy Spirit, the alone unpardonable sin, permit of its identification with the grieving away of the Spirit through a simple indifference to His claims and strivings as is so often represented in the preaching of today?

There is manifestly a difference between a state of confirmed indifference and one of malicious and hateful antagonism, though both are evidently phases of the same moral obliquity, and in harmony with the discussion of this subject as set forth in the preceding pages, a negative answer we feel should be given to the above question.

Gurlitt characterizes the blasphemy against the Holy Spirit as "contemptuous indifference to what is divine and holy." Just wherein lies the exact point of transition between sin of lesser culpability and the blasphemy against the Spirit no mortal mind can ever tell, but contemptuously declaring in the face of the clearest and most convincing light, the redemption of Christ, the things of the Spirit to be matters of indifference, to be, in fact, foolishness—who will say that such a thing is not of sufficient culpability in itself to merit the judgment of blasphemy against the Holy Spirit? But this is different from that simple indifference to the claims of the Spirit, which continues increasingly in the lives of so many about us until they are at last seemingly lost to all impression.

That a high degree of spiritual enlightenment is necessary to the commital of the blasphemy against the Spirit we have already seen, which fact is clearly set forth by such Scriptural passages as are descriptive of it, and some have argued, and not without force, that under such circumstances simple indifference is impossible; a clear conception of moral good implies an imperative; to be convicted of the truth, they say, demands its acceptance or its wilful and scornful rejection.

Again, others have stoutly contended against the thought that a man through simple indifference can ever become completely insensible to spiritual impression. To whom is it given to say? But that simple indifference may so culminate, seems to be reasonable, merely as the result of natural law in the spiritual world. That law is, if a man will not see, he shall not see.

The neglect to use a faculty for its God-given purpose means its final atrophy. One need not break his arm to destroy its powers; simply tie it to the side and leave it there long enough; bandage the eye long enough and it will lose forever its power to see; stop the ears long enough and they will become soundless forever; harden the heart long enough and it will lose forever its capacity to feel. If this is true and a man becomes "past feeling," Eph. 4: 19, through continued indifference, although his condition would be equally hopeless with that of the blasphemer of the Spirit (and for this reason so many have identified them), the distinguishing feature would be not alone in the nature of the states in question, but that the blasphemy against the Spirit, as seen in the case of the blaspheming Jews, is characterized in its outward expression as the fruit of a malicious disposition, while this other has its reference solely to the condition of the man himself.

It is evident whether we identify or distinguish the two forms of sinfulness under discussion that one is equally as fatal as the other, and it is certainly true that sinful development in the case of every sinner must, unless arrested by Redemption, complete itself in such a condition of soul as forever settles the sinner's doom.

> "There is a time, we know not when,
>   A place we know not where,
> That marks the destiny of men,
>   For glory or despair.
>
> There is a line by us unseen,
>   That crosses every path;
> The hidden boundary between
>   God's patience and His wrath.
>
> To pass that limit is to die,
>   To die as if by stealth;
> It does not quench the beaming eye,
>   Or pale the glow of health.
>
> The conscience may be still at ease,
>   The spirits light and gay;
> That which is pleasing still may please,
>   And care be thrust away.
>
> But on that forehead God has set
>   Indelibly a mark—
> Unseen by man for man as yet
>   Is blind and in the dark.

And still the doomed man's path below
　May bloom as Eden bloomed—
He did not, does not, will not know,
　Or feel that he is doomed.

He knows, he feels that all is well,
　And every fear is calmed;
He lives, he dies, he wakes in hell,
　Not only doomed but damned.

Oh, where is this mysterious bourne
　By which our path is crossed;
Beyond which God Himself hath sworn,
　That he who goes is lost?

How far may men go on in sin?
　How long will God forbear?
Where does hope end and where begin
　The confines of despair?

An answer from the skies is sent:
　'Ye that from God depart,
While it is called to-day, repent,
　And harden not your heart!'"

BIBLIOGRAPHY

Barnes, Albert, *Barnes' Notes on the New Testament.* Grand Rapids: Kregel Publications, 1962.

Baxter, Ronald E., *Gifts of the Spirit.* Grand Rapids: Kregel Publications, 1983.

Baxter, Ronald E., *The Charismatic Gift of Tongues.* Grand Rapids: Kregel Publications, 1982.

Bengel, John Albert, *New Testament Commentary.* 2 vols. Grand Rapids: Kregel Publications, 1982.

Bickersteth, E.H., *The Holy Spirit.* Grand Rapids: Kregel Publications, 1976.

Bickersteth, E.H., *The Trinity.* Grand Rapids: Kregel Publications, 1976.

Bullinger, E.W., *Word Studies on the Holy Spirit.* Grand Rapids: Kregel Publications, 1985.

Gardiner, George E., *Corinthian Catastrophe.* Grand Rapids: Kregel Publications, 1975.

Gaussen, Louis, *Divine Inspiration of the Bible.* Grand Rapids: Kregel Publications, 1971.

Marsh, F.E., *Emblems of the Holy Spirit.* Grand Rapids: Kregel Publications, 1974.

Owen, John *The Holy Spirit, His Gifts and Power.* Grand Rapids: Kregel Publications, 1977.

Unger, Merrill F., *New Testament Teaching on Tongues.* Grand Rapids: Kregel Publications, 1974.